SCHOOL DISCIPLINE
The Art of Survival

by

William Allan Kritsonis, Ph.D.
Northwestern State University

and

Sam Adams, Ph.D.
Louisiana State University

LAND AND LAND
PUBLISHING DIVISION

BATON ROUGE, LA
The Book People

School Discipline: The Art of Survival

Copyright © 1986/87, *National Forum of Educational Administration and Supervision Journal*. All rights reserved. Printed in the United States of America. Published by LAND and LAND Publishing Division, 196 South 14th, Baton Rouge, LA 70802. Except as permitted under the United States Copyright Act of 1976, no part of this professional publication may be reproduced or distributed in any form or by any means, or stored in a data base or retrieval system, without the prior written permission of the NFEAS JOURNAL Editor, William Allan Kritsonis. Reviewers who wish to quote brief passages in connection with a review written for inclusion in professional journals, magazines, newspapers, television, video cassette recorders or radio broadcasts may do so as long as proper credit is given to the authors and NFEAS JOURNAL.

ISBN 0-935545-01-8

Library of Congress Cataloging in Publication Data

Price: $10.00

Contents

Introduction v

PART ONE   Background for Understanding
Discipline Problems
- Chapter 1   Discipline Problems 3
- Chapter 2   The Psychology of Misbehavior 10
- Chapter 3   Social Problems and Discipline 17
- Chapter 4   The Principal's Role in School Discipline ... 24
- Chapter 5   Legal Implications and the Handling of Discipline Problems in Schools 31

PART TWO   Solutions to Lingering School Discipline Problems
- Chapter 6   Types of Anti-Social Behaviors in Schools. *What Is the Problem?* 49
- Chapter 7   Reasons for Student Behavior Problems. *Why Do They Act That Way?* 53
- Chapter 8   How Teachers Can Avoid Contributing to Discipline Problems in Schools. *Could I Be Part of the Problem?* 58
- Chapter 9   "If You Can't Control 'em, You Can't Learn 'em." *What Can Be Done?* 65

Suggested Readings 72

Introduction

SCHOOL DISCIPLINE — The Art of Survival contains valuable techniques that are practical. The book is intended for principals, teachers, parents, school superintendents, school board members, professors, undergraduate and graduate students, governmental agencies and many others interested in all aspects of schooling.

A purpose of the book is to strengthen the common bond among people that are responsible for schooling in helping them to survive by providing a new perspective in solving many lingering problems. Another underlying purpose of this book is to help school leaders, teachers and parents to work cooperatively, productively and as a unified voice by providing a new perspective to school discipline and the art of survival.

> WILLIAM ALLAN KRITSONIS, Ph.D.
> SAM ADAMS, Ph.D.

Part One
Background for Understanding Discipline Problems

Chapter 1
Discipline Problems

Our concern is human behavior, or more specifically, human misbehavior. While we focus primarily on the kind of conduct that causes discipline problems for the teacher, we often have to look beyond the immediate school setting in order to gain a perspective regarding such problems.

Discipline Problems Are Not New

When did people start misbehaving? We have a classic description from biblical sources. Adam and Eve were disobedient. Eve consorted with an evil companion (the serpent), yielded to temptation, then prevailed on Adam to eat forbidden fruit. Thus they became "too wise for their own good." And every form of misbehavior seen in this example is still being encountered by teachers on a daily basis.

And who could forget that classic case of sibling rivalry between Cain and Abel? True, our students seldom become so involved in jealousy as to commit murder, the basic components of the Cain-Abel problem are still much in evidence in some class situations.

In the early American schools, keeping order was an endless problem. In part, this was the fault of the system. For example, in the time-honored one room school, the usual pattern of instruction was one-to-one. This meant that each student received a few time-pressured minutes of instruction (more likely, recitation) each day. The rest of the time the student was just there,

3

with plenty of opportunity to create problems. When we add to the situation the further complications of over-age students, often in combination with a very young teacher, we can see that misbehavior was practically inevitable.

The almost universal prescription for dealing with misconduct was corporal punishment. The traditional birch rod was an integral, even vital, tool for "teaching." Often an attempt to whip an older student led to a fight between teacher and pupil; the outcome determined whether the teacher stayed or left. If he lost the battle, this loss often constituted his "letter of resignation."

However, as early as the 1800's some writers were urging a down-grading of punishment as a means of maintaining order. For example, in Hall's *Lectures to Female Teachers,* published in 1832, the author stressed methods that did not involve punishment. He dealt with such suggestions as reasonable assignments, impartiality, organization and student responsibility as means of heading off crisis-type behavioral situations.

Discipline Problems as Viewed by New Teachers

Anyone who works with people occasionally meets a behavior problem — on the part of somebody. However, such problems seem to take on special meaning within the school setting. And they are "especially special" with the beginning teacher. Why is this true?

Students Try Out a New Teacher

Since the time of Adam and Eve, people seem to feel obligated to explore the restraints within which they operate. This is true of school-age people as well as adults. To a class, a new teacher represents an unknown quantity relative to his or her behavior standards. How are students to find out what is expected of them if they don't do some exploring? This exploration usually takes the form of some type of questionable behavior on the part of those students who, by their very nature, seem to feel an obligation to take the lead.

DISCIPLINE PROBLEMS

Seeing in print such explanations as that in the above paragraph is of little help or comfort to a distraught young man or woman who is suddenly beset with doubt as to his or her ability to cope with a spate of behavior problems. However, if the new teacher can preserve a reasonable perspective about the situation, things frequently start to improve after a brief try-out period. There may be a temptation to set behavior standards at an unrealistic level for a while; however, most teachers find it easier to relax a bit than to go the other way.

Incidentally, many new teachers, upon encountering their first discipline problems, react by becoming very critical of the teacher education program from which they recently graduated. Maybe this criticism is, to a degree, justified. But realistically, how *could* you have been prepared in advance for this situation? We are still seeking answers to this question.

Many New Teachers Try Unrealistic Approaches

A veteran teacher recalls that, in his undergraduate education courses, he had memorized the five steps to maintaining class order. But when he got in his own class and faced the inevitable behavior problems, he couldn't remember the five steps. Perhaps, if he had recalled them, these steps would not have been realistic for his situation.

There are certain patterns that usually prevail as the new teacher tries to cope with behavior problems. Some of them go the *dignity* route. This teacher is inclined, by demeanor, to proclaim that I am an adult, a college graduate, and I know a great deal more than you know. Students generally are not notably impressed. In fact, there might be a special challenge for these students — the challenge to "bring him down a peg."

Other new teachers try *threats*. Most students are not awed by the threat of dire consequences that will inevitably follow the next infraction.

Another approach is to *ignore* the infraction. This denies the students the right to establish the restraints within which they are to operate. The result is often chaos.

The New Teacher is Unfamiliar With the Local Situation

Another factor that enters into the situation with respect to the new teacher is lack of knowledge about the local situation.

SCHOOL DISCIPLINE

For example, although there is debate about this, if the new teacher knew something about the students in advance of classroom contact, some problems might be averted. Do you think a new teacher should be briefed regarding known troublemakers? Would this lead to a self-fulfilling-prophesy situation?

Also, the new teacher may be unclear as to sources of help in dealing with behavior problems. Some principals encourage office referrals; other discourage them. Some more experienced colleagues are willing to give informal assistance (at least moral support!) while others have a completely different attitude about it. Only by working in the situation for a while can the new teacher begin to understand how things are done.

New Teachers Often Feel Insecure

Any new situation is fraught with problems, real and/or imaginary. And the new teacher is especially susceptible to a feeling of insecurity, since *everything* is new. This feeling is immediately sensed by students, and many of them stand ready to exploit it to the fullest extent possible.

One result of this feeling of insecurity is a tendency for the teacher to over-react to problems that arise. Any offense becomes a "hanging crime." Under these circumstances, punishment is likely to be swift, and unrealistically severe. If the teacher is inclined to introspection, he or she is likely to be overly self-critical of the way in which the problem was handled. And there is always the possibility of a loss of poise, leading to temper tantrums or tears, neither notably effective in coping with the problem.

Where Are New Teachers Likely to Work?

Most fairly large school systems have a variety of assignments, ranging from milennial to purgatorial. From the standpoint of logic, it would make sense to assign new teachers to the easier situations until they make some adjustments to the role of the teacher. But this is seldom done. The new teacher is likely to be assigned to "more challenging situations." One reason is that, because of high turnover rates, the vacancies are likely to occur in the more difficult situations. Also, the new teacher, anxious to get started on a career, is not likely to engage in ex-

DISCIPLINE PROBLEMS

tended negotiations regarding job assignments. One administrator, faced with the task of staffing a particularly difficult school, said that, when he sent a new teacher there, he felt that he was presiding at a sacrifice. However, many new teachers survived the process, and some actually came to like working in this type of school.

Discipline Problems and the Experienced Teacher

If one wanted to paint a rosy picture regarding discipline problems, he could say that such problems disappear as the teacher gains experience. Many of the situations described earlier will likely clear up as the teacher becomes more familiar with the work of teaching. However, unfortunately, some teachers never seem to make any real gains toward the goal of effective discipline.

Even the most insightful teachers with years of experience in the classroom occasionally find themselves in the position of having to cope with behavior problems.

Some teachers have, over the years, developed the knack of recognizing potential trouble spots in advance. Usually such teachers can avert a crisis situation by taking a few simple, unobtrusive steps. Often this can be as simple as a change in seating patterns or a minor re-working of a time schedule. This ability cannot come from reading books; it comes from time spent in actually working in the school setting. And, to some teachers, it never comes.

Solutions to Discipline Problems Are Being Sought

If we accept the fact that discipline is a problem in many schools — and how can we deny it? — we are professionally obligated to try to find solutions to the problem. Many groups are trying.

Many teachers, who are on the firing line day after day, ponder the question constantly — not in terms of principles or generalizations, but in terms of individual students or small groups of students. Such teachers investigate home situations, seek for hobbies or interests through which a student might be approached or confer with other teachers or administrators. As

7

SCHOOL DISCIPLINE

in any problem solving process, complete information is most important.

Also, many groups of teachers work on the problem. For example, faculty study meetings in some schools are devoted to a considerable extent to the discussion of problems and — hopefully — solutions in the area of behavior. Formal organizations of teachers often give attention to behavior matters through the establishment of committees and commissions.

A school administrator at any level is likely to be involved in disciplinary matters, both with immediate action and with the long-range goal of finding solutions to problems. For example, a principal might observe that a certain teacher seems quite comfortable with ninth grade groups but has discipline problems with the older students — say twelfth graders. Often, through a change of assignment, the situation can be improved. Also, the principal seeks solutions through all sorts of administrative practices. Is there a best time for a student assembly? Are football games turning into riots? How should class parties be supervised? The list is practically endless.

School boards are often deeply involved in disciplinary matters, particularly at the policy level. For example, in a particular school system, a long sequence of disciplinary problems arose in a particular high school because dress regulations, left to the discretion of the principal, appeared to be unduly restrictive. A special aspect of the problem was that the principal at a neighboring school had no such regulations. The school board intervened and set up a committee of administrators, teachers, parents and students. This group was charged with the responsibility of setting up a dress code. Their code was approved by the board and served as a baseline for principals. This largely alleviated the problems that had grown up in the school whose principal had insisted upon rigid standards of grooming.

Parents are also seeking answers to behavior problems. The type of misbehavior that occurs at school is likely to carry over to the home situation. Often the parents turn to the school for help in understanding their puzzling progeny. In a vast majority of cases, success in developing proper conduct on the part of students is promoted by a joint effort between home and school.

8

Also, solutions to many types of behavior problems are being sought through the courts. While most judges admit to a lack of expertise in the area of student behavior, circumstances often force the judge to be actively involved. For example, the decision to send a problem student to a correctional school (often misnamed!) is usually made by a judge. Too, many extreme behavioral problems such as riots often end up in court.

What Is the Role of the Teacher?

Throughout this book, emphasis is placed on the role of the teacher in keeping order within a classroom, since this is where the teacher spends most of the school day. However, other problem areas do exist. For example, many fights seem to develop in the lunchroom or on the playground, possibly because large numbers of students congregate there. Also, for the teacher there is hall duty, bus duty, assembly duty — the list is long and varies from one school to another. And each locale is a potential source of discipline problems.

One point is worthy of emphasis regarding these out-of-class situations, *viz,* what is the teacher *supposed to do* under various circumstances? For example, what are the ground rules to be observed on the playground or in the lunchroom? Many new teachers actually contribute to problems because they have not been adequately briefed as to role and function. Also, an important question is: What should I try to handle on my own, and what should be referred to others? In short, the teacher who is "pulling duty" needs to have a clear concept of the proper way to handle situations that may arise.

IN CONCLUSION

Behavior problems are as old as people. In the school setting, new teachers, experienced teachers, administrators and others are in continuous contact with various aspects of the discipline problem. A few basic principles apply to all: (1) know the facts relative to the infraction, (2) know the rules, legal and otherwise, that apply, and (3) do not take action while angry, under emotional stress or while suffering from fractured dignity.

Chapter 2
The Psychology of Misbehavior

One teacher at an inner city school explained, somewhat ungrammatically, that "When you're looking down a gun barrel, you're not likely to be thinking about no psychology." Another said of a particular student, "That boy was born to raise hell and psychology's got nothing to do with it." Both points of view, at least on the surface, appear to have some merit. However, if we consider that psychology deals with behavior, and since our concern is with behavior, the two domains must overlap at some points.

No attempt is made in this book to re-hash any major segments of formal psychology. Rather, certain aspects of psychology that seem to bear directly on student behavior will be considered in the applied, rather than the theoretical, sense.

Most teachers have had some courses in psychology. However, this background is usually quite inadequate to justify such teachers in efforts to solve single-handedly complex psychological problems among students. Yet any effort to cope with behavioral problems on the part of teachers is likely to be more effective if such teachers have a fair degree of understanding of some basic psychological principles.

Why Do Discipline Problems Arise?

The list could be very long; however, we will deal only with certain problems that are encountered daily by classroom teachers.

Boredom

One might challenge whether boredom really relates to psychology. However, because boredom is vitally involved in classroom behavior, it is included here.

The pioneer teacher in America tried to teach all of his students on a 1-to-1 basis. When increasing enrollments made this impossible, there was a reaction which followed this line of thought: We will cluster our students in rooms of 25 or 30 and assign a single teacher to teach them. These students will all be of about the same chronological (not mental) age. The teacher will teach all of the students the same material at the same time and at the same rate.

Under these circumstances the teacher took the logical route and geared his instruction to the "average" student. This meant that the high performance student had completed his assigned work in a very short time, and, unless the teacher made provisions for him, was now faced with a massive spare time problem. Then the teacher had an opportunity to observe that the high-speed mind which allowed this student to complete work in record time was equally effective in dreaming up ingenious ways to create behavior problems.

Frustration

In the situation described above, another type of student was in even greater trouble, *viz*, the low performer. The pace of instruction that was geared to the middle-range performers simply ran away and left the low-performance student behind. To add to his problem, this student plodded along year after year, incurring ever-increasing deficits. For example, before he had become proficient in addition, the class moved to subtraction; before he mastered multiplication, the class started division. After a certain time, the teacher was trying to "teach" this student material he could not possibly learn because of gaps in background.

Frustration can lead to a wide variety of behaviors. For example, Judy, upon learning that she would likely have to repeat fourth grade, simply retired into her own world in which such distasteful matters as arithmetic and spelling could be eliminated. Joey, a more direct type, would rip pages from his book if they contained troublesome content. And Pat, direct to the point of violence, would hurl his book at any likely target across the room.

A particularly unfortunate aspect of frustration is the way in which well-meaning people may add to it. For example, a teacher who hints in her most tactful manner that, unless Mary's work improves, retention in her grade level is likely is simply adding an element of fear to existing problems. And the parent who points out, "Your *brother* was an *excellent* student" is not likely to produce any positive results.

One type of reaction to frustration is to quit trying so as to have an alibi for failure. In the minds of many students, the verbalization of "Of course I failed; I didn't crack a book!" sounds much better than, "I tried but still failed."

Rebellion

Rebellion can be a reaction to many types of situations. It can range in intensity from a simple lack of participation to a wild, screaming fit. And rebellion is encountered among all grade-level groups. Amy, a cooperative third grader, suddenly found herself having to share the attention of her parents with a baby brother. Almost overnight, she changed into a troublemaker, both at home and at school. The resentment was not directed against the new baby but against the adults whom she identified with her now-threatened world.

We generally associate rebellion with the adolescent years, and indeed, in many situations, this becomes a major problem. At this age, many students are very impressionable, and worship at the shrine of peer acceptance. So, if the peer group decides not to take baths for a while, the usually-docile Sally and Bobby horrify parents and teachers by skipping baths. This even carries over into academic achievement. The once-good student decides that he would be more popular if he makes failing grades — which he then proceeds to do. One father, who had not had the benefits of a formal education, said of his adolescent son, "He ain't got a brain in his head!"

Some teachers view rebellion as a student's way of asserting his individuality, and these teachers frequently work through this type of behavior with a minimum of disruption. Other teachers, inclined to be somewhat less understanding, seem to live in a state of continuous confrontation with their students. This latter situation is obviously very wearing on all concerned.

Insecurity

The way in which people react when their security is threatened varies widely. Amy's reaction, cited earlier, was partially due to the fact that the arrival of a baby brother caused her to have doubts as to her status in the family. Such cases are very common in the work of teachers.

The sad case of Judy illustrates the same situation. An attractive, popular teen-ager, Judy was very fond of her father. He died very suddenly as Judy was entering her junior year in high school. After a period of intense mourning, Judy suddenly became very different from her former self. Shortly she was experimenting with drugs, sex, and every sort of deviant behavior. A quickie marriage came and went. A distraught mother felt utterly helpless in the situation, and school personnel, while deeply concerned, could offer little help. The situation ultimately cleared up, at least in part, as Judy finally established herself in a new world that did not include her father.

Many teachers have had the experience of working with children during the time when their parents are getting a divorce. The ways in which these children react to this situation (to them, the ultimate insecurity) vary widely. Some rebel; some withdraw; some manage to feel a degree of responsibility for the situation. And some assume patterns of classroom behavior that are utterly foreign to previous patterns. Certainly a student who is undergoing such a traumatic experience needs and deserves a great deal of understanding on the part of teachers and other school personnel.

One other case was that of Jane. The oldest of several children, she grew to the age of 12 in a home in which the mother did not hold outside employment. Then the mother accepted a job in a hospital, her work hours being from three until eleven at night. Not only was Jane's security threatened by the loss of a full-time mother; Jane was expected to assume major responsibility for her younger siblings. Her teachers almost immediately noticed a change in Jane. As a result of a need for reassurance, she constantly talked about her new role — always in a complaining way. Even more of a problem was the fact that Jane was now deprived of the attention from adults that she had formerly had. Her reaction was to demand extra attention from her teachers, and she would use any tactics, reasonable or unreasonable, in order to gain the attention for which she hungered.

Where does the list of psychologically-based behavior problems end? Every experienced teacher can extend it to great lengths. Once we identify some of the underlying factors of discipline problems, then what do we do?

How Do We Help?

An understanding of the background relative to a behavior problem can only help. Yet if we understand and make no effort to do anything about it, what purpose is served?

Obviously it is impossible here to list a step-by-step procedure by means of which we could cope with disciplinary cases. Yet there are a few basic approaches that might contribute to solutions.

Accept the Fact That Performance Varies

The basic fallacy of trying to teach all members of a class in total cadence has been described. How *can* we work around this problem?

The High Performance Student. This potentially valuable asset to society will live in a state of boredom unless provisions are made to prevent this. After he has achieved the basics, why not give him a chance to "spread his wings" with a special assignment of some sort? To be effective, this work must be truly challenging, not just more of the same. Further, it must be in an area of interest to the student (and not necessarily to the teacher). It should culminate in some form of recognition — a display, a report, a publication or something along this line. It would not necessarily tie in directly with what the class is doing but, for maximum effect, it should relate to current class work. One secondary mathematics teacher will challenge a high performance student to find alternate ways for carrying out certain operations; to develop mathematical proofs of well-known procedures; or to see how much of the solution to a problem he can carry "in his head."

A word of caution is probably in order about our work with this student. There is always the temptation to use him as a handy man and errand runner simply because he can spare the time. This is not fair to the student, since he is meeting the teacher's, rather than his own, needs. Further, in an era when peer tutoring is being recognized as an acceptable teaching procedure, there is the possibility that, unless careful attention is given, the high performance student will become a full-time tutor — again, because he has time to do it. While a certain amount of work along this line might serve a useful purpose, this student should not become an unpaid teacher aide.

The Low Performance Student. The behavior problem on the part of this student likely relate to frustration, as previously discussed. But doesn't every student have a right to be successful, at least occasionally? Obviously, if this student is to ever experience the joy of achievement, it will have to be in terms of differentiated assignments. A basic principle is that we must locate the point of entry for this student, then start him at that point. Sometimes this can be worked out in an unobtrusive manner, expecially with younger students. However, it becomes more complex with junior and senior high students. Yet many teachers manage to make the differentiated assignment work at these levels.

The low performance student is likely to have had little or no recognition — for anything. Yet recognition seems to be a basic hunger in our makeup. As part of the general approach described above, many teachers seek ways in which honest commendation can be bestowed upon the student. Sometimes this type of recognition has to be based upon non-academic performance. One fifth grade boy in this category used a pen knife to carve a bird out of a piece of soft wood. The teacher had him show it to the class and answer questions about it. Then she borrowed it so it could be kept on display in the classroom. The impact on the student was tremendous. This was accentuated by the fact that this boy seldom encountered anything except criticism at home.

SCHOOL DISCIPLINE

Be a Human Being

Many of the factors that contribute to behavior problems lie totally outside the school setting, as illustrated earlier. There is nothing the teacher or principal can do about a totally disruptive home situation, or the fact that the student lives in a crime-ridden neighborhood. However, it *is* within the power of the teacher to be open and accepting in his or her dealings with the student. Even very young children sense and react to rejection; nobody could truly enjoy being rejected. Yet many students have encountered little else outside of school.

There is a narrow line between being interested and being nosy; between being courteous and being solicitous. Yet, to be effective in the area of human relations between teacher and student, the teacher must locate and observe these distinctions.

Give Students a Part in Rule Making

Whether we call them rules or something else, any social group such as a classroom must have behavior guidelines. Such rules can be in the form of edicts handed down in an unilateral manner by the teacher, and indeed this is a very common practice. However, many teachers try to bring the students in on any discussions related to the rules under which they are to live. In some classroom situations this probably would not work; some teachers would have difficulty in using this approach even if the class cooperated.

The merit of some system which allows for student input in the rule-making function is obvious: It is not the teacher's rule; it is *our* rule. Under these circumstances, students frequently take an active part in enforcement, which tends to minimize the "you *versus* me" atmosphere.

IN CONCLUSION

All behavior, constructive as well as destructive, is caused. The teacher may not have the background and does not have the time to try to engage in a detailed psychological analysis of each behavior problem. But if the teacher can develop the skills needed to recognize boredom, frustration, insecurity and other such factors, he/she can often use them in constructive ways.

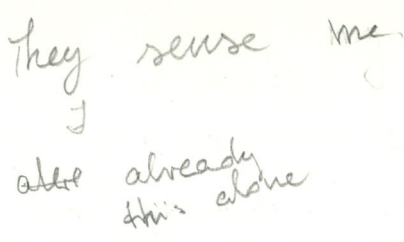

Chapter 3
Social Problems and Discipline

Again, no attempt will be made in this chapter to cover the broad and growing field of sociology. A brief survey of certain sociological principles that have specific impact on the work of the teacher — and more specifically, on student behavior — will be attempted.

Some Problems Relate to Sociology

Urbanization

For most of its existence, America was predominantly rural. A farm economy was the standard pattern. Although there were many drawbacks, there were many strengths in such a system. A youngster grew up in an atmosphere of basic security. His or her role in the family, community and school was fairly clear. The children had assigned responsibilities from an early age, and most of these kept the child working in close proximity with parents, grandparents, siblings.

As families moved to urban areas, the pattern described above underwent a drastic change. The family wage earners went their separate ways, and many children were not clear as to where the father worked or what he did. And even the very young children felt a sense of vague insecurity because subsistence depended on the pay check. In times of high unemployment, an extra strain of worry was added.

A rural family transplanted to an urban area often experienced strain because of crowding, the mere presence of people close by. This alone resulted in emotional stress.

The role of children underwent a change in the urbanization process. On the farm, large families were an asset, as there were never enough hands to do what needed to be done. In the urban setting, children became economic liabilities in that they had to be fed, clothed and attended to with little hope of becoming contributing members of the family group until they reached maturity.

What impact did these changes have on a child's behavior at school? He was faced with an overwhelming adjustment. The size of the school was awesome; the teacher remote; the students sophisticated in all sorts of questionable practices. Under these circumstances the student might become excessively shy, retiring to a dream world; or he might set out to earn a place in new surroundings by becoming louder and more hostile than even the most blase city dweller. Either response was of real concern to the teacher.

Family Changes

As a result of a variety of social and economic forces, the role of the family has undergone major changes in recent years. The family unit has lost much of its identity, again with a resultant loss of security on the part of the youngsters. For example, the stern, inflexible father, while possibly lacking in warmth, provided clear guidelines for youthful behavior. Such guidelines were periodically breached by children; retribution was swift and sure. But such guidelines are now recognized as a basis of secure feeling on the part of children. Indeed, reasonable discipline in whatever form is often associated with security.

The home in which both parents hold jobs, a relatively recent development in America, has created its own type of sociological problems. Reduced parental supervision of children is often a direct result of both parents working outside the home. There is less association with parents in terms of time. Often the parents, worn out from the day's work, are not very congenial company when the family is together. One principal recently complained that, in his school, he had great difficulty getting parents to come to school on major disciplinary cases involving suspension or expulsion. The reason was simple: both parents worked in most families, and a trip to school meant the loss of a day's work.

SOCIAL PROBLEMS AND DISCIPLINE

Even more difficult for many students is the ever-growing problem of one-parent households. With divorce becoming more and more common, many youngsters are facing the problems of less supervision and more responsibility that go along with the one-parent household. Of course, the divorce statistics tell only part of the story. In many situations, a parent simply disappears from the scene without bothering with such details as divorce or child support. This adds still another variable to the life of the children involved.

Obviously all sorts of problems based upon insecurity, rejection or even abuse are brought to school by children from the homes described above. Added to these are the fact that many children may see in the teacher a mother figure or a father figure. This can bring about a severe emotional drain on the teacher, with attendant problems.

The Job Situation

In earlier years, a student who had little aptitude for or interest in "book larnin" simply dropped out of school at an early age and went to work on the farm. In an urban setting, however, he is unemployable until he reaches the minimum age according to applicable laws. This has served to make many schools at the upper grade levels into human warehouses where teachers attempt to cope with "in-school dropouts." Many modern-day discipline problems originate with this group of "students."

Another feature of the problem described above is that, even after the student reaches an employable age, jobs are very hard to find. The minimum wage level as established by law is such that employers constantly seek ways to eliminate the more menial jobs. A case in point was a food processing plant that employed about a hundred people all with minimal skills. The time came when the minimum wage rate became so high that the owner automated his plant. After that, he employed only three people all of whom were well trained and highly skilled.

These comments should not be construed as being of a negative tone relative to child labor or minimum wage regulations. But if we look at them solely in terms of their impact on schools and teachers, we can readily see that some problems have been generated by the enactment of these laws.

What does the teacher do who finds himself faced with a substantial number of in-school dropouts who are simply putting in time? The teacher should get all the help that is available from the administrative and supervisory staff, develop a tough skin, and keep trying. This is one of the most serious discipline problem areas in many schools today.

Mobility

In addition to the farm-to-city movement mentioned earlier, there is endless movement among Americans. Major corporations often transfer employees across country. Career military people are often involved in transfers. And many other segments of the population seem to love being in motion. One youngster, son of a corporation executive, attended almost 20 schools during his 12 years of elementary and secondary work. He reacted by becoming a major scholastic and behavior problem. Many smaller children revert to earlier habits such as thumb sucking when the family moves.

There can be no question that a youngster goes through a period of trauma when he is moved — with a family, from one divorced parent to the other, from one foster home to another, or however. An understanding teacher can be of a great deal of help to a child during the resulting period of adjustment.

Parental Attitude Towards School and Teachers

The school is often a focal point, a social center, a source of pride, in a rural community. Further, teachers are usually well-regarded as among the best-educated people in the community. Leadership roles in the community are often assumed by school personnel. In this setting, parents are usually inclined to push education for all it is worth within their own families. Also, there is often the comforting feeling that teacher knows best. In case of a discipline problem with a student, the teacher can generally count on parental support in coping with it. Under these circumstances (and such schools still exist), discipline is of minimal difficulty.

But these circumstances, once common, are being encountered less frequently. Many parents (possibly because they don't know their offspring very well) almost automatically support their children whenever there is conflict between teacher and student. Perhaps the fact that the teacher is often a totally unknown person enters into this. Also, the fact that the student is unlikely to give the parent an objective description of the situation is doubtless a factor. Whatever the reason, home and school are often at odds in coping with behavioral problems involving today's students.

Similar attitude changes have occurred regarding schools and education generally. In earlier years, many parents saw education as the pass key to a better, easier life. Today many blue collar workers, often with high school educations or less, have better incomes than do many college graduates. Under these circumstances many parents are not notably enthusiastic in their support of high academic achievement on the part of their children. In short, schools as social institutions are not held in the high regard that they once were. This has had a considerable impact on the degree of devotion — or lack of such — found among students for education. This, in turn, has undoubtedly had an impact on student behavior in the classroom and on the playground.

Changing View Toward Authority

Some students, notably adolescents, have always been inclined to challenge authority. This applied to all authority figures, including teachers and parents. However, for the past two decades or so, there has been a greatly accentuated trend in this direction — and not just on the part of teen-agers. Riots often involve participants from every conceivable age group. In many cases, the triggering incident is minor in nature, but in practically all riots, the anger is directed toward authority figures, usually law enforcement personnel.

An attitude bordering on contempt for authority has infused many student groups and continues to make trouble for school personnel. Theories abound as to why this change in attitude has occurred. Most teachers do not have the time or, in some cases, the inclination to try to locate the basic causes; they are too busy trying to cope with the resulting changes in their classes.

Racial problems frequently contribute to the type of situations described above. These often defy any system of logic. Many schools with multi-ethnic populations go along for years with a minimum of problems, only to have problems appear quite suddenly, frequently over relatively minor issues. One school official attributed a major racial outbreak to an election of cheerleaders. He said he wished all the vicious behavior elicited could have been concentrated in the football team!

How Do We Help?

Most of the sociological factors described earlier lie in areas that are completely outside the control of the teacher. What, then, can we do when problems arise? A few points are worthy of note; perhaps you, on the basis of your experience, can add to this list.

1. Try to understand the problem. This is basic to any type of problem solving, behavioral or otherwise. What would *you* be like if you were in the student's circumstances? From this point, common sense is the best guide. When John, a handsome seventh grader, became hostile and openly defiant, a concerned teacher looked into the background. She found that John's father was incurably ill, that his mother had to work to support the family, and that the latter added to the problem by feeling very noble over her role. Just knowing of these conditions helped the teachers help John through a difficult period of life.

2. While being understanding, avoid being solicitous. This approach arouses resentment and often contributes to the problem.

3. Learn to listen. Many students of all ages are hungry for an attentive, adult listener. Perhaps some of the deviant behavior we encounter is a bid for someone's attention. A teacher, in order to be an effective listener, has to avoid the temptation to correct language usage, possibly profanity. One writer has said that the greatest compliment you can pay a person is to give him your full attention. This must be good therapy, since entire professions are based on it.

4. Don't try to settle everything yourself. Many problems are too big for the teacher to handle unassisted. For example, if a major racial incident breaks out, the teacher is very restrictive as

to what actions to take. Perhaps the best approach is to call the appropriate authorities, then "do a discreet fadeout." There is little purpose served in your becoming a dead or seriously injured hero!

5. If there are specific ways in which you can render service, you should do it; but don't try to take on the problems of the world. A sociological problem that has been developing for a hundred years is not likely to yield to the ministrations of a single person.

6. Be observant. Most discipline problems are the culmination of an extended growth period. Many times a teacher who observes the trend can intervene in an unobtrusive way and head off a confrontation.

IN CONCLUSION

Changes in society have had a tremendous effect on schools and the attitude toward authority that students of today exhibit. Such areas as urbanization, family changes, high unemployment and others impact on people, especially school-age people. Although teachers cannot control these changes, they can make an effort to use them constructively. A first step in this direction is to try to understand the problem.

Chapter 4
The Principal's Role in School Discipline

This book deals with the teacher as the central figure — not the principal. The principal is endlessly involved in dealing with discipline problems, but his role is somewhat different from that of the teacher. Indeed, a large volume of published material deals with the technical aspects of discipline as they apply to the work of the principal. Yet in many respects the teacher and the principal work as a team on major discipline problems. This chapter emphasizes the role of the principal as viewed by the teacher.

The Principal Is a Helper

Most principals readily concede that they cannot unilaterally maintain discipline in Miss X's classroom. However, as popularly quoted, the head person in any organization sets the tone for the total operation. Hence, in the ideal situation, the principal and other administrators establish the policies and guidelines dealing with discipline, and the teacher applies these within the classroom, on the playground or wherever problems arise. Logically it should follow that the teacher has the full support of the principal in the process. (What does the teacher do if this support is not forthcoming? The answer is still being sought.)

Responsibility
The teacher needs to understand the role of the principal in disciplinary matters. The principal of a large school has one of

THE PRINCIPAL'S ROLE IN SCHOOL DISCIPLINE

the most complex jobs society has to offer in that this principal is technically and, to a degree, legally responsible for everything that goes on in the school. So, while Miss X is "bending his ear" about the misbehavior of a particular student, the principal might well be dividing his attention between her problem and such matters as a losing football season, bickering between certain teachers and complaints about the quality of the food in the lunchroom. In the background might be concerns over bigger issues, such as the threat of a riot in the gymnasium, a pending suit over charges of discrimination, and a disagreement with the superintendent over accounting methods.

The purpose of this description is to point out that, although the behavior problem with Johnny is of paramount interest to the teacher, this is one of the many problems facing the principal. There is little to be gained by delaying the teacher-principal conference until another day. The principal's "worry list" will change but it is always lengthy.

Many teachers who take pride in thinking and speaking in positive terms about people make a single exception — the principal. Perhaps if these teachers had a clearer concept of the complexities of the principal's role, they would be less likely to complain that, "I didn't seem to have his full attention."

Self Interest

Any professionally oriented principal wants good order to prevail and will do his utmost to help bring this condition into being. He knows, for example, that a single uncontrolled class has an impact throughout the school. Students are adaptable, but going from a near-riot situation to a more formal setting is a big change — and often creates problems in the new setting. Hence, as a simple matter of minimizing problems for all concerned, the principal would like to eliminate the disorderly situation that is generating these problems.

The principal's own self-interest is best served when good order prevails. While the charge is sometimes heard that "They made him a supervisor because he couldn't handle a principalship," generally professional advancement comes to those who have performed well in other areas. Hence the principal who is known to run a good school is usually given careful consideration when promotions are being made.

In many schools telephones are found only in the central office. There are those who say this is a doubtful blessing. But when a school in general or a specific teacher is having problems in the discipline area, the phone in the principal's office gets a real workout. In short, if there are complaints, they usually go to the principal first. Again, from the purely practical approach, the principal's self interest is best served when things are running smoothly at school.

Some of the above comments might seem somewhat negative in tone. This was not intentional. However, in a purely positive sense, the principal should be interested in promoting the best possible learning situation. A part — a very important part — of this learning situation is good order in classrooms and all other phases of school operations. This can be achieved only through a team effort involving principal, teachers, and staff.

Position

Because of the nature of his job, the principal is usually in position to be uniquely helpful in the discipline area. As a counselor to teachers, for example, he can often head off trouble. Recently a first year teacher came to the principal in a great state of agitation because some of her second graders had cheated on a spelling test. In the rashness of her own youth, she was in the mood to make "a federal case" of it. She was personally affronted, and in her conference with the principal, she kept repeating such terms as, "I simply will not tolerate cheating in my room." The principal donned the role of counselor and, through calm discussion, gradually led the young teacher to see that rash action was not the best course to take. If she had thrown around a few drastic statements (her first inclination) with some name-calling, the principal's telephone would have gone into action almost immediately.

After a principal has worked in a school for a few years, he should be fairly well informed as to special circumstances that bear upon student behavior. Often some information as to family situation, community background and related matters can help the teacher see a problem or a potential problem in its true frame of reference. Hence, the teacher can frequently learn

THE PRINCIPAL'S ROLE IN SCHOOL DISCIPLINE

a great deal about a situation from the principal. Obviously, for this information to serve a useful purpose, it should be acquired *before* the teacher has taken action on the problem.

Another role for the principal is in the general area of school law. While presumably the principal is not a lawyer, still a person in this position would likely accumulate a certain amount of information as to what teachers are and are not allowed to do under existing laws. For example, is corporal punishment permissible? If so, under what conditions? What are local and state regulations dealing with school attendance? Suspension? Expulsion? What recourse is available to the teacher against whom a legal action is filed? Is it legal to post grades, or does this violate the privacy of the student? The knowledge of the principal in these and similar matters is the first line of defense for the teacher. If there are indications that the teacher may be involved in a sustained period of legal action, an attorney is needed. Even here, the principal would likely know of attorneys who are especially knowledgable regarding this type of action.

The Principal Is an Enforcer

Many times the application of school policies as they relate to discipline is placed directly in the hands of the principal. It follows logically that the principal should be brought into the situation before the enforcer role is brought into play. Obviously the principal is placed in a very awkward position if, by the time he learns of a problem, it has grown to crisis proportions, without his having had any sort of opportunity to help avert the "showdown phase."

The same general idea applies in referrals to specialized personnel or agencies. Obviously, chaos would be the result if each teacher in a large school made his or her own referrals to the psychologist, social worker, or to juvenile court. Generally such referrals are made by the principal, although needy cases would be brought to his attention by teachers.

As an illustration of the principal's role in the discipline area, let's look at a set of regulations pertaining to corporal punishment. (This is a slightly modified version of an actual set of regulations as adopted by a school board).

— The principal will have the option of using corporal punishment. Corporal punishment will not be used in a school without the approval of the principal.

— Specific behavior which warrants corporal punishment must be outlined in the Administrative Handbook . . . Corporal punishment may be used only after less drastic deterrents fail.

— Corporal punishment shall be administered only by a principal or assistant principal in the presence of another member of the professional staff of the school.

— Corporal punishment shall be administered only after obtaining written permission from the parents or legal guardian and such permission shall be kept on file in the principal's office.

— The student shall be advised of the misconduct of which he is accused and the basis for such accusation and shall be given the opportunity to explain his . . . version of the facts prior to the imposition of corporal punishment. In cases where applicable, the student shall be given a choice of corporal punishment or suspension.

— A record of each incident of corporal punishment shall be kept which shall include the name of the student and the time, date and details of the violation, the form of discipline administered and the name of the person administering the discipline and the witnesses thereto.

— The official who has administered the corporal punishment must provide the child's parent, upon request, a written explanation of the reasons for this form of punishment and the name of the other professional staff member who was present.

— Nothing contained in these regulations shall be interpreted as prohibiting an employee from using physical force, reasonable and appropriate under the circumstances, in defending himself against a physical attack by a student or to restrain a student from attacking another student or employee or to prevent acts of misconduct which are so anti-social or disruptive in nature as to shock the conscience.

— The official administering corporal punishment shall do so in a reasonable manner, taking into consideration the age, size, emotional condition and health of the student.

— In the event a suit is brought against the principal or administrator, the school board's legal counsel, the district attorney, or other counsel selected or approved by the board will represent and defend.

In many phases of the disciplining process, the principal is designated by law or by board policy as the person who assumes ultimate responsibility, including punishment, suspensions and referrals. However, if the role of principal is to be workable, this official must have the support and assistance of faculty members.

There is often a temptation for the teacher to be critical of the principal regarding his role of disciplinarian. He is accused of being too easy. An often heard comment in the teacher's lounge starts with, "If I had his job for just 15 minutes, I bet I could . . . ." Yet the teacher who finds criticism of the principal to be a favorite indoor sport usually has much less information about a problem situation than does the principal. A case in point: While the offense may merit suspension, the principal knows that, while under suspension, the student in question will be totally unsupervised, roaming the streets, consorting with known criminals. What, in such a case, is to be gained by a suspension? So the principal desperately seeks other ways to handle the case.

The Principal Is a Referrer

According to state law in many states, only the principal can refer a student to other agencies. Under these circumstances, the principal is likely to maintain good communications with the other agencies in question. He knows, in an informal way, which agencies are most effective in rehabilitation, which are adequate for "storage." In short, the principal is likely to be reasonably well informed as to the best procedures to use in meeting the special needs of special students. This is valuable information in situations where a variety of approaches is available.

The task of referral is not taken lightly by most principals. One such official remarked that any time he had to enlist the help of an outside agency, he was admitting defeat on his own part. Hence, referrals are usually made as a result of a calm exercise of judgment — not emotion. A particular teacher hauled a hapless youngster to the office and demanded that he be referred then and there to the juvenile authorities. When asked about her complaint, she said he was ungovernable — and repeated the demand that the referral be made. The principal found that this teacher was the only one who had trouble with this lad, and a simple change of schedule took care of the situation.

IN CONCLUSION

In the modern school the role of the principal is very complex. As applied to behavior problems, he is helper, enforcer and referrer. An effective program of discipline can be implemented only when the teacher and the principal work in a team effort. The teacher who is critical of the principal as he functions in discipline should bear in mind that this is only one of the many areas of responsibility for the principal.

Chapter 5
Legal Implications and the Handling of Discipline Problems in Schools

The day when school personnel had a wide degree of latitude in dealing with problems in the area of pupil behavior is definitely past. Litigation in this phase of school operations seems to be endless. No attempt will be made in this chapter to present anything of a "final" nature, since new laws — and new judicial interpretations of existing laws — are constantly changing the picture. Also this discussion will emphasize those legal aspects that have relatively direct bearing on the work of the teacher.

In a decision on a well-known case that ultimately went to the United States Supreme Court, the following position was established: "Students in schools as well as out of schools are persons under our Constitution. They are possessed of fundamental rights which the state must respect, just as they themselves must respect their obligations to the state." School boards are constantly studying their positions relating to pupil behavior in the hope that they can establish policies and procedures that will stand the test of judicial review. Numerous local, state and national organizations are working on guidelines for use by school boards. In some cases these guidelines go beyond existing law in the direction of protecting student rights, since the trend of court decisions seems to be in the direction of more such protection.

What Is Due Process?

A great deal is heard about due process as applied to the students' rights in disciplinary actions. The terms seems to mean different things to different people. However, in a general way as applied to students, it seems to mean that clear, definite and fair rules or procedures must govern disciplinary actions. This leaves no room for hasty or impetuous action on the part of school authorities; there is no place for an instant rule.

As an illustration we will take the matter of suspension from school for disciplinary reasons. Some requirements that apparently must be met relative to due process are:

(1) Violations that may lead to supension must be listed, and the list must be available to students.

(2) The pupil must be given an opportunity to express himself relative to the alleged offense.

(3) With minor exceptions, no student may be released during the school day without notification of parent or guardian.

(4) Written notice to the student and parents as to reasons for a proposed suspension must be provided within a brief period of time after the offense (for example, one day).

(5) Within two or three days a hearing must be held before a school administrator. This hearing involves students and parents; an attorney may or may not be present, depending on local rules. This hearing is technically more of a counseling session than a judicial hearing.

(6) After the hearing the parents and student must be notified in writing as to whether the student is suspended, along with reasons and conditions.

(7) The student is notified as to when he can return to school.

Obviously the teacher who descends upon the principal's office demanding that a particular student be suspended forthwith and immediately is not likely to prevail. Due process as applied to students makes such an action practically impossible.

Laws Deal With Several Areas

Legal rulings have been made regarding a wide variety of student activities — questionable content in the school newspaper, wearing arm bands as a form of protest, and on and on. Here we shall examine several areas that are more directly applicable to the work of the teacher.

Search and Seizure

As to searching a person, the same rules seem to apply to students and to non-students. A "rule of thumb" which has thus far been accepted is that the search of a student's person should be carried out only when the administration has reasonable belief that the student is concealing evidence of an illegal act or school rule violation. Even this seems to be continuously litigated, and changes as to legal status may occur at any time.

Considerable attention is being given to such matters as search of a student's locker. This seems to be an area of continuing interest. An earlier ruling held that, since the locker is provided by the school and is technically the property of the school, this locker can be searched by school authorities without a warrant and without the consent of the student. This ruling further held that contraband found during such a search could be used as evidence for court proceedings. However, many school systems have carefully avoided full use of the prerogatives thus granted and search lockers only under carefully prescribed conditions.

Perhaps the classroom teachers will have little occasion to engage in search and seizure. Yet several major court tests have been based upon acts by classroom teachers rather than administrators.

Dress

Who can forget the era when boys grew long hair and teachers grew indignant? This era was also marked by a general change in dress practices, with girls showing up at school in miniskirts or overalls. Many school boards loaded school administrators with completely unenforceable rules. If the principal had taken all of these directives literally, he would have spent all of his time measuring the longness of the hair and the shortness of the skirt.

While an effort was made by the courts to balance student rights against other considerations — academic, health and safety factors, for example — student rights have consistently won out. Dress is considered a matter of personal self expression, and rigid rules have been consistently voided. Many school systems are now making student dress and grooming a matter to be determined by students and parents. Some sets of regulations make certain specific exceptions; others leave the matter open-ended, with major responsibility assigned to the principal.

Meanwhile some teachers still feel that they are being affronted unless certain dress standards are met by their students. A word of caution is: Don't engage in unilateral action; don't try to use a set of standards that varies from that of the school system. Such a practice can only lead to ill will and ultimate defeat.

Corporal Punishment

About half of the states have laws that deal, in one way or another, with corporal punishment. However, many school systems have regulations banning corporal punishment, even in states whose laws permit it.

Of course, corporal punishment was considered an integral part of education for many years. The "board of education" hung on a nail behind the teacher's desk in thousands of classrooms. However, there has long been a continuing discussion as to the effectiveness of this practice. Some teachers see the use of the paddle as an admission of failure; others see it as "speaking to him in a language he can understand."

In situations where corporal punishment is an accepted practice, there is usually a carefully precribed procedure to be used. The teacher who thinks there is a possibility that this type of punishment may be invoked should carefully check with school authorities regarding these procedures. And a cardinal principle is never administer corporal punishment in anger. This has led to innumerable damage suits against teachers, and in a substantial number of cases, the ruling was against the teacher.

How Can We Operate Within the Law?

Many school systems have used court rulings and other guidelines in order to draw up statements relative to discipline in their own schools. Following is a composite example. A large number of publications by school systems have been examined, and this illustration closely patterns after many of them. Thus far, the general approach represented here has been found to be legally acceptable.

DISCIPLINE POLICY

School discipline has two broad objectives. Fair and impartial discipline helps insure a proper climate for learning and it also helps students develop the self-discipline that is required for all learning.

Although the ultimate responsibility for student conduct rests with the student and his parents, it is the daily responsibility of school personnel to see that no single person interferes with the total learning environment of other students.

Individual human conduct is a composite of many factors which teachers cannot always overcome during the school years; therefore, when the student fails to discipline himself to follow the established rules of school, it becomes the school's responsibility to discipline the student.

As prescribed by law, every teacher is authorized to hold every pupil to a strict accountability for any disorderly conduct in school or on the playground of the school or on any street, road, or school bus going to or returning from school, and during intermissions or recesses. It is the final responsibility of the principal to maintain discipline at each school.

Schools do assume a responsibility to help a student learn self-discipline. However, when a student exhibits marked deviation from acceptable behavior, it is the responsibility of the teacher, principal, guidance, attendance, and psychological personnel to undertake every effort to identify the problem, to secure parental understanding and cooperation, and to help the student in accordance with their best judgment and the resources available.

In those cases where corrective action becomes necessary, the disciplinary measures taken should be positive, constructive, and directed toward serving educational ends. It should be clearly understood by the student and his parents that the purpose of all disciplinary action is to mold future behavior and to teach the student that education is a right qualified by compliance with reasonable rules and regulations.

While the school is concerned with the individual and his welfare, it must also be concerned with the group and their welfare by preserving the proper atmosphere for teaching and learning.

Deviations of behavior shall result in attendance at student clinics or by suspension and/or expulsion. Students who have been denied normal attendance privileges because of suspensions or expulsions for more than twenty (20) days, may seek attendance at specialized schools.

MINOR OFFENSE REGULATIONS

A. *BEHAVIOR CLINIC* (For Junior-Senior High School Students Only)
  1. When students commit minor offenses, it is recommended that teachers contact, by phone or otherwise, the parents and inform them of the problems before referring the students to the principal.
  2. The student remains in class until seen by the principal. The principal may: counsel with student; administer punish work; refer student to the guidance counselor, or refer the student to a behavior clinic. He should contact parents, if possible, and request a conference. Written communication to parents concerning the discipline problems is advised.
  3. The clinic provides an alternative to the routine procedure for dealing with disruptive students. Its operation is based upon the concept of positive intervention behavior modification theory and techniques. Alternative forms of the clinic may be used when deemed necessary by the principal.

  Failure to appear at clinic on the assigned date will result in a suspension unless the student has a valid excuse. *Students with valid excuses must attend make-up sessions of the clinic at the next session. The Behavior clinic will be conducted after school for a period of at least one hour and forty-five minutes.* Students may attend clinic for only four offenses. Suspension will occur with the fifth offense.

Parents will be informed of assignment to the clinic.

B. *CORPORAL PUNISHMENT*
1. Corporal punishment is defined as punishing a student by striking on the buttocks with a paddle provided by the School Board a maximum of five (5) times. Such punishment must be administered in a reasonable manner taking into consideration the age, size, emotional condition and health of the student.
2. Corporal punishment shall be administered only by a principal, assistant principal, or teacher after having obtained permission from the principal. Such punishment shall be administered in a specific place designated by the principal and in the presence of another member of the professional staff.
3. Written permission must be obtained from the parents prior to the administration of corporal punishment and kept on file in the principal's office.
4. The student shall be advised of his/her particular misconduct and shall be given an opportunity to explain his/her version of the facts prior to the imposition of corporal punishment.
5. A record of each incident of corporal punishment shall be kept which shall include the student's name, and the time, date, details of violation, form of discipline administered, the person administering such discipline, and the witness. Upon request of the parent, the principal shall notify the parents of such violation and punishment.

ELEMENTARY SCHOOL REGULATIONS

Elementary school principals may use, at their own discretion, any of the junior and senior high school discipline regulations they feel advisable. However, the following student offenses should draw a conference with the parent and/or social worker, followed by a short-term suspension on the second offense:

Disrespect for authority
Disobedience
Cursing faculty or school officials
Threatening faculty
Vandalism
Extortion

OTHER OFFENSES

Other offenses established by other written regulations of the School Board or adopted by the principal of a particular school and approved by the Superintendent of Schools shall be punished in accordance with the punishment set forth in such regulations.

An accumulation of offenses at one occurrence may result in the taking of more severe disciplinary action, such as a short-term or long-term suspension.

Any student who deliberately refuses to obey the request or directive of a teacher or school administrator during disruptions will be suspended. Further refusal to leave the school premises after this suspension will result in calling in law enforcement officials, and students will then be arrested as trespassers.

A weapon is defined and classified as any form of object that may be used to inflict physical damage upon another person.

Discipline problems on the school bus will be dealt with by the principal of the school responsible for the student in accord with state laws and school regulations. Principals will take action necessary to insure operational safety of the buses.

SUSPENSION REGULATIONS

A. Suspension from school can be one of two types:
   1. *Short-Term Suspension* is any denial of school attendance for five days or less.
   2. *Long-Term Suspension* is any denial of school attendance for a period in excess of five days but not beyond twenty (20) days.
B. When, in the judgment of the principal, the clinic is not proving to be a successful deterrent to misbehavior, the principal may suspend. Evidence of this would be numerous clinics for various offenses. Students may attend clinic *for*

only four offenses, with suspension starting with the fifth offense.

SHORT-TERM SUSPENSION PROCEDURES

1. Principals must make every reasonable effort to investigate all aspects of a discipline problem. If the principal finds the offense is of the nature that demands suspension, the student should be suspended.
2. Prior to any suspension, the school principal shall advise the pupil in question of the particular misconduct of which he or she is accused as well as the basis for such accusation, and the pupil shall be given an opportunity at that time to explain his or her version of the facts to the school principal or his designates.
3. The principal shall make every effort to contact the student's parents or guardians by telephone, if possible, notifying them of the suspension, and that the student will be or has been removed from his class and will be kept under supervision until the close of the school day or the arrival of the parent or guardian. If the parent or principal so requests, the student will be granted an early dismissal from school to return to his home. In the event a student may cause a disruption of the orderly operations of the school, he may be removed from the school premises immediately and placed in the custody of his parents or next of kin.
4. The principal will mail a report of the suspension to the parent or guardian preferably on the day of the suspension, if possible, but no later than the following school day. Additional copies shall be sent to the Superintendent's office, the Office of Child Welfare and Attendance, and the guidance office of the school. In addition, the principal or assistant principal shall keep a copy on file.
5. If the parent or guardian of the suspended student wishes to contest the suspension, the parent or guardian, within five (5) school days after receipt of written notification of the suspension, may submit a written or personal request to the Superintendent to review the

matter. Upon such request the Superintendent or his designee shall schedule a hearing at his earliest convenience to be held in accordance with the hearing procedure described within the context of the long-term suspension procedure.

REINSTATEMENT OF STUDENT ON SHORT-TERM SUSPENSION

Upon the student's return to school, if the results of a prior conference have not been successful, the principal shall schedule a conference to be attended by appropriate school personnel and by the student and the student's parent(s) or guardian(s).

If in the judgment of the principal the response of the parent(s), or guardian(s) is deemed necessary for the student's successful reinstatement to the school, and the parent(s), guardian(s), or other family member fails or refuses to respond, the principal may recommend a long-term suspension to the Superintendent.

WARNING

After three short-term suspensions, the next occasion warranting any form of suspension shall result in recommended expulsion. The same notification procedure as other short-term suspensions shall be issued with the exception that the written notice to the parent will be sent by certified mail, return receipt requested. The student and parent or guardian shall be informed, by verbal and written communication, that any subsequent occasion warranting any form of suspension, after the third suspension, shall result in recommended expulsion.

LONG-TERM SUSPENSION PROCEDURE

1. Principals must make every reasonable effort to investigate all aspects of a discipline problem. Principals shall have reasonable cause to believe that the student is guilty of an offense which would constitute grounds for disciplinary action and that the situation warrants severe disciplinary action before recommending to the Superintendent that the student be placed on long-term suspension.

LEGAL IMPLICATIONS

2. Principals shall determine, according to the nature and the seriousness of the offense, whether a student recommended for long-term suspension may remain in school or be denied attendance rights pending a hearing. (A hearing must be scheduled on all long-term suspensions. If the student is denied attendance, this fact shall be stated on the recommendation.)
3. If the principal denies the student attendance rights pending a hearing by the Superintendent, the principal shall make every effort to contact the student's parents or guardians by telephone, if possible, notifying them of the impending suspension and that the student will be or has been removed from class and kept under supervision until the close of the school day or the arrival of the parent or guardian. If the parent or school so requests, the student will be granted an early dismissal from school to return home.
4. Serious disruptions may cause the student to be removed from the premises immediately in the custody of his parents, next of kin, or police.
5. Official notification of suspension shall be made to the parent or guardian no later than two (2) days following the incident with copies to appropriate school officials.

SUSPENSION HEARINGS

1. The school shall notify the parents or guardian of the suspension hearing date and the action to be taken if the parent is not present. The hearing will take place not later than five (5) school days after the incident.
2. If suspension proceedings are conducted without the presence of a parent, written notification of the actions will be sent by certified mail to the parent not later than three (3) school days after the hearing.
3. Parents wishing someone else to represent a student must notify the Superintendent in writing twenty-four (24) hours before the hearing.
4. Until the matter is reviewed by the Superintendent, the student will be denied attendance privileges.

SCHOOL DISCIPLINE

5. The parent or guardian may appeal the suspension to the School Board within five (5) school days after receiving notification by certified mail. In so appealing, the parent shall enclose a copy of the principal's recommendation for a long-term suspension and the Superintendent's notification after the hearing. The School Board will review the appeal and take whatever course of action they deem appropriate and will so notify the parent of their decision. In the absence of a timely appeal, the decision of the Superintendent shall become final.
6. After two long-term suspensions, the third occurrence during the same school year which warrants a long-term suspension, will result in disciplinary action in accordance with the expulsion procedure.
7. Upon the student's return to school, the principal shall schedule a conference to be attended by appropriate school personnel and by the student and, usually, the student's parent(s), guardian(s), or other family member. Follow-up conferences should be planned as indicated or required to assist the student in adjusting to the school environment.

EXPULSION PROCEDURES

1. A principal shall initiate proceedings for an expulsion when a student has received two long-term suspensions in one school year, and the principal has reasonable cause to believe that the student has committed a third offense in the same school year which might otherwise warrant a long-term suspension.
2. After a principal has made every reasonable effort to investigate all aspects of the discipline problem and is satisfied that the nature and seriousness of the offense warrant the ultimate form of disciplinary action, he shall recommend to the Superintendent that the student be expelled from the school system.
3. The principal shall make every effort to contact the student's parents or guardians by telephone, if possible, notifying them of the proposed expulsion and that the student has been removed from his class and either kept

under supervision until the close of the school day or the arrival of the parent or guardian, or placed in police custody. If the parent or school so requests, the student will be granted an early dismissal from school to return to his home.

4. The principal will mail a report of the proposed expulsion to the parent or guardian on the day of the student's removal from school, if possible, but no later than the following school day. At the same time the principal shall notify the parent or guardian of the time, date, and place of the hearing. This report will be sent by certified mail, return receipt requested.

5. Where the Superintendent has proceeded with the expulsion hearing without the parent being present, he shall give written notification to the parent of his findings and action taken no later than three (3) school days after the hearing. In such notice the Superintendent or his designee shall inform the parent that the findings and action shall become final by ten (10) calendar days.

6. The hearing shall be held as soon as possible but no later than eight (8) school days after the student's removal from the school, unless a later date is agreed upon by all parties concerned. In the event the parent wishes someone else to represent the student, he or she must sign a statement to this effect.

7. Pending the hearing by the Superintendent, the student shall be denied attendance privileges.

8. At the hearing conducted by the Superintendent or his designee, the reason concerning the cause for the proposed expulsion is to be presented by the principal in support of his recommendation. The student's prior performance and attendance may also be discussed. The student may present evidence or whatever else is appropriate in his behalf.

9. The student and his parents are entitled to representation by another person of their choosing, including legal counsel. Such representative shall have the rights of full participation in the hearing as in the long-term suspension procedure. School personnel are afforded the same

SCHOOL DISCIPLINE

opportunity.

10. After hearing the case, the Superintendent or his designee shall find whether the student is guilty of the principal's charges. In accordance with such findings, he may administratively transfer, suspend, or expel for a limited or unlimited time, if so recommended by the principal. He may otherwise employ other lesser disciplinary measures he deems best suited to the case.

11. If the findings and disposition of the expulsion hearing are made at the conclusion of the hearing, the Superintendent shall inform the parents and the student of his findings and disposition of the case. In any event, the Superintendent shall mail or hand to the parents (by certified mail, return receipt requested), to the Child Welfare and Attendance Section, and to the principal, no later than three (3) school days after the hearing, a written notification of his findings and what action will be taken. In the event of an administrative transfer, a copy of the written notification shall be sent to the receiving school.

12. In the event the student is expelled, the parent or guardian of the expelled student may appeal the Superintendent's decision to the School Board. The appeal must be made within five (5) school days of the Superintendent's decision and must be requested by certified mail.

13. The parent or guardian of an expelled student may, within ten (10) calendar days, appeal to the district court for an adverse ruling of the School Board in expelling the student.

14. Students would be expelled for the remainder of the school year. Students expelled during the first semester who desire to return at mid-term may make a request to the Superintendent's office where the request will be evaluated. Students returning at mid-term will return on probation.

STATUS AND REHABILITATION OF SUSPENDED AND EXPELLED STUDENTS

During the period of suspension, the student who is denied attendance privileges should be kept at home during school hours.

In no case should he be allowed on School Board property without prior authorization. Participation and presence of the suspended student at school extracurricular activities is denied. The student who is allowed to remain in school pending a hearing by the Superintendent is considered to be on probation. Additional violation of school rules will result in loss of attendance privileges until the case is resolved at the hearing.

The necessity to suspend or expel a student usually indicates that additional support and remedial services are necessary. The principal and professional staff have a responsibility to provide proper counseling and to make every effort to help students returning from suspension and expulsion to remain in school. Suspended students will not be allowed to make up work for period of time suspended.

The preceding section was presented in detail to illustrate the length to which school systems have gone in trying to comply with legal requirements in the area of school discipline. How times have changed since the day of the freely-applied "board of education!"

IN CONCLUSION

Obviously the time when a teacher could function as prosecuting attorney, judge, jury and executioner is gone. Indeed, such terms as "due process" are part of the vocabulary of many students. A detailed knowledge of the legal aspects of school discipline is not required of the teacher, especially since this area is undergoing constant change. But it is important for the teacher to understand that the rights of students are being "protected" as never before. The logical move is to ask for help when questions arise, before taking any action that might be questionable or unlawful.

Part Two
Solutions To Lingering School Discipline Problems

Chapter 6
Types of Anti-Social Behaviors in Schools
What is the Problem?

A teacher in a frontier community once remarked that, "If you can't control 'em, you can't learn 'em." Hence, he spent much of his time in keeping order, or, as he called it, dis-*cip*-line. Of course, his main tool was the birch rod, or corporal punishment.

This teacher's axiom, "If you can't control them . . ." has much truth in it. The situations change, and our approaches in dealing with them change. But, unfortunately, the basic problems of classroom control persist. Veteran teachers still suffer with the beginner as he — young, confident, idealistic — gropes toward the development of his own skills in keeping order in a class. Meanwhile, the veteran teachers are also coping with the ever-changing problems.

Our purpose here is to be very basic and practical in our approach to discipline. However, a 1-2-3-4-5 procedure will not work; there is no formula. As a point of departure, let's take a brief over-view of the problem of keeping order.

The Basic Problem Is Anti-Social Behavior

There are many kinds of behavior that our society does not condone, and we have massive volumes of laws reflecting this. The school is a microcosm of the society that supports it, and one role of the school is to educate students as to acceptable behavior. Isn't the kind of behavior we as teachers object to also unacceptable outside of school? Let's look at a few of these types.

Vandalism

America's schools are spending many millions of dollars each year because of vandalism. What could be in the mind of a person who engages in sheer, pointless, profitless destruction? Some writers in the field speculate that vandalism is a revolt against authority, and that the people involved associate the school with authority. Others say that frustration and failure in school tasks build resentment against school — resentment that is expressed through broken windows and smashed furniture. There are other theories, but nobody knows for sure just why school vandalism is such a mammoth problem.

Fighting

In some settings, fighting is looked upon as a simple matter of self-expression. In these situations as long as nobody gets seriously hurt, a fight is considered to be a minor infraction. Yet, whatever the setting, fighting is classed as an anti-social activity and is to be dealt with as a disciplinary problem. One veteran teacher recently remarked that, as long as his students fought each other, he wasn't too disturbed, but that more and more they wanted to fight with him. It is a matter of record that thousands of teachers are physically assaulted by students each year. This obviously cannot be shrugged off as a minor phenomenon.

Classroom Disruption

The list here could be quite long-throwing chalk, books, erasers, spitballs; being unduly noisy; even speaking out of turn. These may sound relatively minor, yet they give many teachers a great deal of trouble. In fact, these are the infractions that "get a teacher down" to a greater degree than most, simply because these problems are ever-present. These will get considerable attention in later chapters.

Stealing, Cheating, and Others

This list has no end, since each experienced teacher could add to it. Some of these incidents occur in the classroom while others may arise on the playground or elsewhere. Frequently, especially with young children, such infractions give rise to a teaching situation in that the youngsters actually don't know about property rights of others. In such cases teaching should precede — or hopefully replace — punishment. Nothing could be more self-defeating than to punish a child for an infraction he does not comprehend.

The Goal is Intelligent Self-Control

We shall not yield to the temptation to be idealistic at this point. Yet there can be no doubt as to our ultimate goal in that phase of education we call discipline. Our goal is to promote growth toward the time when our students will behave properly *when they are not being watched.* This can take a variety of names, but the concept is simple. When viewed in this light, we see discipline as being a part of social and emotional growth, indeed, a vital part of it; we see teachers as key agents in the promotion of such growth. This is in contrast to the earlier concept of the teacher as being endlessly engaged in doling out punishment. Penalties still have a place, but hopefully they are being used primarily as teaching devices, not just for punishment.

In our efforts to promote growth toward intelligent self-control, we are not functioning alone. The influence of home and community is a major factor. Sadly, the school often teaches values and methods that do not parallel those being taught by the other agencies. This can lead to endless confusion in the mind of a youngster, and this confusion often leads to behavior problems. We as teachers cannot change home conditions, but it is often helpful if we know about them.

We Take Students As They Are

A major factor in the discipline problems confronting the teacher is this: The teacher did not have the opportunity to select his or her clientele. We take our students where they are, as they are, not "where we wish they were." Nothing is more futile than for the teacher to day-dream about the good situation that would be possible if a few students could be palmed off on someone else. Very few teachers have any influence in the matter of student selection, so we have no choice but to take them as they come to us. But self-control is a learned skill, and in learning we build on a base of "where we are."

So as we start each new year, gazing at class lists, then at faces, we are likely to view a choice collection of complexes, "hang-ups," levels of achievement, personality conflicts, and on and on — and they are all ours!

IN CONCLUSION

What is the problem? Basically, the problem is that we work with people. People are complex, confusing, often undisciplined. A teacher's approach to a discipline problem can take on a positive tone if the teacher keeps in mind that the goal is to help the student develop intelligent self control. This accentuates teaching rather than punishment.

Chapter 7
Reasons for Student Behavior Problems
Why Do They Act That Way?

We as teachers cannot set ourselves up as authorities in psychology or psychiatry. Yet, as people who work with people, we need to be aware of some of our own quirks, as well as those of our students. An often-cited principle is "all behavior is caused." When we are confronted with a disciplinary crisis, we are not likely to react in an analytical manner, looking for basic motivations. But frequently, if we will recognize the true nature of our students, we can forestall a crisis. Hence, we should give some attention, in a practical rather than theoretical way, to the basic question as to why our students act the way they do.

1. *The students feel an obligation to try out the teacher.* In any social system, people are unsure as to the restraints under which they are functioning until they try them out. This is quite applicable to a classroom setting. Have you ever noticed how a group of students will be rowdy and noisy in one teacher's class but will be just the opposite in the class of another teacher? These patterns were likely arrived at by simply testing the situation.

2. *Certain students are not interested in the material being studied.* It is most unlikely that any student is equally interested in all phases of his work. Yet a person would get a rather lopsided education if he only worked on areas of interest to him.

We as teachers have to accept the situation and work with it as best we can. In a small high school, a young shop teacher was having all kinds of behavior problems. Upon investigation, he learned that, because of the school's limited offerings, many of his students were taking his course solely to get the required number of units for graduation. He was able to make some simple adjustments in the classwork and thereby increase the course's appeal to more students. His discipline problems reduced correspondingly. You can imagine the problems encountered by a wide-eyed, idealistic young English teacher as she tried to get a class of boys (sole interest: basketball) to appreciate the finer points of "Paradise Lost."

The logical question as to this problem is: What do we do about it? This varies widely according to the local situation. But a first and vital step is to recognize that the problem exists.

3. *Everybody needs recognition as a person.* With many people, the need for attention from others is almost a physical hunger. And if this needed attention is not provided as a result of constructive efforts, some people will switch to other tactics — any tactics — in order to get attention.

Sometimes this need is especially prevalent because of home background. One fifth grade boy went to the office and complained that his heart was hurting. He made it sound very serious. A school nurse could find no basis for his ailment — except that he was number seven in a family of 13! The "heart problem" was a method of getting some attention from adults. In another family there were two brothers who were a year apart in age. The older boy was "Mr. Everything," an outstanding athlete, student and leader. The younger brother could not gain any recognition along these lines, since he could not successfully compete with his brother. He got his attention by becoming a major discipline problem.

How can this be dealt with in a classroom? Care should be taken by the teacher to see that every student is periodically recognized for something he has done. At times this can be a real challenge!

4. *Some problems have an academic base.* We all give glip lip-service to the "individual differences" idea. Yet we are still seeking the best way to teach individuals while working with

large groups. There is the tendency to rely heavily on group instruction, and the teacher is likely to gear the level of instruction to the so-called average student.

This practice invites problems, especially from two groups: (1) the high performance students who find themselves bored and unchallenged because they are being "taught" something they already know; and (2) the low performance students who are being called upon to work at a level completely beyond their present competence. The teacher is dealing with some students who are bored and with others who are frustrated. Inevitably such students will use misconduct as a means of voicing their dissatisfaction with the situation.

An illustration of the frustration aspect described above happened in a fourth grade arithmetic class recently (a true case!). The teacher returned a ditto worksheet to a boy with the comment, "They are all wrong. Do them over." In the absence of any instruction, he would logically have done them wrong again. The student threw a book across the room. Can you blame him?

5. *Many students are born conformists.* The fear of being different is very strong in some people. It is said that students at the junior high level are especially motivated toward conformity. But whatever the age group, the argument that everybody else is doing a certain thing can be very persuasive, even if the act in question is known to be undesirable or unlawful. One group of junior high girls was engaged in shoplifting. The items taken were of little value and all of the girls came from fairly affluent homes. The actual value of the stolen articles was of no consequence. The sole explanation was that the girls were playing follow the leader, with the fear of being called "chicken" overriding all other considerations.

In a classroom, the general tone can be such that even the best students engage in all sorts of questionable activities, yielding to the call of conformity. The task of the teacher is to change the tone by any means that are available.

6. *Many students bring resentments to school.* A teacher can be overly sensitive about student behavior. After all, the school is only one of the many influences to which a student is subjected. A human life is not neatly compartmentalized. The stu-

dent with whom we work brings to school many attitudes — some positive, some negative. The high school boy who, at breakfast, had a major argument with his parents over the use of the family car will likely arrive at school in a foul mood. This results in negative attitudes or even disruptive actions at school.

Cathy, an attractive ninth grade student, was usually cooperative and cheerful. However, on certain days, she would be totally different — sullen, rebellious, rude. Her teachers learned that, when Cathy was wearing "that look," they would not call on her for anything. Through discreet inquiry, the counselor learned that Cathy's father was an alcoholic, and Cathy's moods coincided with his periods of heavy drinking. The axiom that "all behavior is caused" was verified in the life of Cathy.

7. *To many youngsters, rebellion is part of growth.* Tearfully the mother of a junior high school boy confided to the counselor regarding the rebellious, even hostile, attitude of her son. Periodically, she reverted to her favorite statement, "and he used to be such a sweet boy." Many parents and teachers have this same experience as youngsters pass through adolescence. And if adolescence is confusing to us, think what it must be to the student!

The change from childhood to adulthood involves all sorts of strange phenomena. The indifferent dresser becomes overly concerned about appearance; the conscientious student becomes a rattle-brain and the docile, accepting student suddenly blossoms out as a flaming rebel. We as teachers deal with this enough that it doesn't bother us unduly. But frequently we have to help the student (and his parents) through this trying period.

8. *Let's face it; some need to be referred to other agencies.* One young teacher had a simple diagnostic statement regarding his problem children: "There's something wrong with that boy (or girl)." In a period of a few weeks, he would apply this description to every student in his class. When it becomes a case of "everybody's out of step but me," the time has come for some self-examination on the part of the teacher.

In our society, we have some youngsters whose needs cannot be met in the standard classroom setting. These students obviously need to be evaluated by specialists, either within the system or through referral. Often the most significant clues to problems are to be found in the area of classroom conduct. The teacher should not try to cope with psychological or emotional problems that require the services of specialists. However, it is equally important that the teacher not over-use the referral process.

IN CONCLUSION

This chapter deals with eight reasons "why they act that way." Can you add to the list? Several of the reasons listed in the chapter are of such a nature that the teacher can actively help the student as he tries to cope. Others are almost totally foreign to the world of the teacher. Probably the chief contribution of the teacher in these areas is to be (1) informed and (2) a good listener.

Chapter 8
How Teachers Can Avoid Contributing to Discipline Problems in Schools
Could I Be Part of the Problem?

Self-evaluation can be a painful process. When a problem arises involving a teacher and a pupil, the teacher will often place total blame on the student. What is the student likely to be thinking? A school administrator remarked that many of the discipline problems referred to him were actually teacher-generated. Would you agree? Another principal says that he can always tell when Miss X is not feeling well; she keeps a parade of students passing through his office.

One teacher described her approach to discipline this way: "When I point one finger at my class, I am pointing three fingers at myself." This is not to imply that the teacher is always in the wrong. Rather, it means that there may be different ways of doing things — ways that might work better. In one classroom, the pencil sharpener was located in such a way that students waiting to use it often got into shoving, elbowing encounters. Instead of punishing the students, the teacher looked the situation over objectively, then moved the pencil sharpener to a better location. The problems cleared up immediately.

Within the general context of teacher self-evaluation, the following list of suggestions is presented. Some of these might logically appear in the next chapter. However, all of them deal

AVOID CONTRIBUTING TO DISCIPLINE PROBLEMS IN SCHOOLS

to some degree with the teacher as a person, hence are included here.

1. *Be organized.* The operation of a classroom is a task in engineering. A key concept in smooth operation is organization. For example, the teacher who takes an inordinate amount of time trying to find things she "put away yesterday" is asking for behavior problems. Housekeeping matters should be routinized so that the prime attention of teacher and student can focus on the teaching-learning process.

2. *Be definite.* Assignments should be spelled out so that students know what they are to do. The amount of guidance required varies with the age and maturity of the students. Any evidences of indecision can serve as the point of entry for misbehavior. Let's look at three different assignments. "And now you may review for a while." "I think you need to review the material on gas law problems, so you may work on this for a while." "During the next ten minutes see how many of the gas law problems you can complete. They are found on page 168 in your book." Any experienced teacher will see the gradation in this sequence. The first one is an open invitation to "goof off," with attendant problems. The second is more definite, while the last is even more so. Student response would likely be more positive in the third assignment.

3. *Be natural.* Even a small child can detect insincerity — and resent it! The story is told of the young teacher who had her class on a field trip for nature study. She patted a tree lovingly and gushed, "Oh, you dear old oak, how I love you!" All of the students knew that it was a maple tree. Another teacher went into ecstasies because Joey had worked a problem in arithmetic. Then Joey's neighbor pointed out that the answer was incorrect. Such over-done incidents make the teacher look silly.

Most students accept teachers for what they are, but the process of developing a functional relationship with students is greatly simplified if we don't try to be something we aren't. We deal with observant people, and any attempt to fool them usually creates problems.

4. *Act your age.* Students do not look upon you as a buddy, pal or peer. They expect you to be a mature adult. They assume that there will be a generation gap. Many young teachers have a

tendency to seek popularity, and in their efforts along this line, they resort to tactics that can create endless problems. While it is true that the real age spread between the teacher and some of the students may be relatively small, two different levels of maturity are represented. One young lady, just out of college, suggested that her senior high students call her by her first name. Almost immediately problems began to crop up. The teacher-pupil relationship is not a peer relationship.

5. *Be consistent and fair.* Students are confused when a teacher accepts a certain type of behavior today but flares up over the same behavior tomorrow. The teacher who can be consistent in day to day relationships with students is at a definite advantage.

Nothing arouses student resentment more than for a teacher to have pets. Historically, the term "teacher's pet" has had a stigma attached, and this is still true. We as teachers are most unlikely to deliberately have pets, but sometimes a pattern of preferential treatment for certain people can creep in. For example, in giving grades, we have two students whose class work is about the same. One is clean, cooperative and pleasant; the other displays totally opposite traits. Wouldn't it be easy to "make an error in arithmetic" in favor of the former?

Some teachers report that consistency and fairness are doubly important in a classroom where two or more ethnic groups are represented. Unless he is very careful, the teacher may be accused of favoritism toward his own ethnic group. When this happens, disciplinary problems are likely to ensure.

6. *Develop a thick skin.* The classroom can be a chamber of horrors for a teacher who is excessively sensitive. Many students come from an environment where blunt, direct or even crude speech is the norm, and any student can on occasion provide an opportunity for the teacher to get his or her feelings hurt. If the teacher is inclined to do so, he or she can live in a perpetual state of pout, self-pity and anger.

Unfortunately, some teachers consistently apply adult standards to student conduct. Such standards are acquired as part of a growth process. In a first grade, a boy was telling about seeing a dog run in front of a car. As he put it, the car "knocked the hell out of the goddam dog." The teacher, after the initial shock, made this a teaching situation rather than a disciplinary case.

Another application of the idea expressed above lies in the question: What shall I see or not see? What shall I hear or not hear? Many times, diminished perception is the best strategy. A young man was working as a counselor at a large inner-city high school. He found that, when he would walk past a group of students in the corridor, there would frequently be a remark made about him (but not *to* him) that could have led to a disciplinary situation. But he developed the ability to ignore these remarks; outwardly, he didn't hear them. After a period of time, the remarks were no longer made, since they had not served the intended purpose.

7. *Avoid arguments.* A teacher who is firm and fair does not move in on a situation until the right time, and this basically means that this teacher knows what is happening. Under these circumstances, it serves no constructive purpose for the teacher to engage in a prolonged argument with one or more students. Let us examine two ways to handle a common situation. Teacher A suspects that, on a test, Paul is trying to copy off Billy's paper. Teacher A observes closely, becomes convinced that her suspicions are true, and unobtrusively moves Paul to a different seat. Nothing is said, and the other students do not even observe that Paul has moved. Teacher B, facing the same situation, airs her suspicions to the class, engages in a lengthy argument with Paul regarding his conduct, then sends him to the principal's office for insubordination. The merits of Teacher A's methods are obvious.

8. *Avoid temper fits.* One mark of emotional maturity on the part of a teacher is that he or she does not yield to the temptation to become angry, yell, and especially to cry. Any experienced teacher has dealt with youngsters who specialized in trying to produce some such reaction on the part of the teacher. What greater satisfaction could one give such a student than to "play the game his way?"

Miss E was a beginning teacher of high school English. She was young, somewhat naive, a bit of a "culture nut." Two senior boys had a way of engaging in conversation about the poem under study, and their remarks seldom reflected credit on either the poem or the poet. Miss E construed these remarks as a reflection on her teaching (exactly what the boys intended her to do) and frequently burst into tears of frustration. She lasted one semester. Her replacement, a much more stable person, treated the situation as a joke, and in short order, this is what it had become. When the challenge to goad Miss E to tears disappeared, the fun was gone.

Incidentally, the question as to why students will act in the way just described is a difficult one. There are always some who will act this way, and the successful teacher learns to work with them. The system that will work best has to evolve, but the system that is least effective is undoubtedly that of pitching a temper tantrum or bursting into tears.

9. *Develop a set of values.* A veteran teacher recently remarked that one of his most important lessons had been that of learning what is important. Some teachers find themselves taking an inflexible stand on issues that are of minor importance, and this is most unlikely to promote a good learning environment. A case in point is Miss Greg, a veteran teacher. When the fad of boys wearing long hair came on the scene, Miss Greg "went in orbit." The school board set a policy regarding hair length and authorized the principal to enforce the policy. Miss Greg blithely ignored this and set her own policy, with herself as prime enforcer. She was in an untenable position but refused to accept the realities of the situation. Innumerable problems ensued — so many that Miss Greg retired early because of this problem, which really was not her problem at all.

Many mathematics teachers find it necessary to remind students to bring pencils to class, since seat work is very important. But Mr. Z went a step beyond reminding; he issued an edict to the effect that any student who failed to bring a pencil would be immediately sent to the office as a discipline case. Can you imagine what happened? The students rose to the occasion. Some days not a single student brought a pencil, with pandemonium the end product. The principal had to intervene and straighten out the situation. Obviously, Mr. Z had succeeded in making a big issue out of a minor one.

10. *Do not threaten.* In a well-organized classroom, students know the standards of conduct they are expected to maintain. When this situation prevails, there is no point in the teacher's harping on the swift and terrible punishment that awaits the transgressor. Probably all teachers at one time or another have to take some sort of disciplinary action. But, provided the student is clear as to the nature of his infraction, there is no point in making threats. If the standard is of such a nature that a violation deserves punishment, then the teacher should punish. There is nothing to be gained by an extended lecture as to what the teacher is going to do when the next violation occurs.

11. *Avoid humiliating the pupil if possible.* If we view our goal as intelligent self-control on the part of the student, then it follows that discipline is an integral part of the teaching-learning process. Actions or remarks that tend to humiliate a student do not promote learning, whether they occur in the area of mathematics, science, or self-control.

In the complex field of human interaction, outcomes are difficult to predict. One teacher might comment on a student's attire in such a way as to amuse the student and his peers. Another teacher might say essentially the same words but evoke a response of resentment and humiliation. The latter teacher would have been in a better position had he or she refrained from making such remarks until a working relationship had been established.

A teacher can use terms relative to the school work, personal habits or even the ethnic background of students in such a way as to produce a violent reaction, to the complete surprise of the teacher. This can happen because certain words mean different things to different people. A teacher in an inner-city elementary school found that certain expressions, quite acceptable to her, had insulting connotations to some students. Think of the disciplinary problems this situation could have generated!

12. *Give the students responsibility if they can handle it.* The extent to which this can be done varies widely. The assumption of responsibility on the part of the student is a growth process and should be encouraged.

One teacher at the lower elementary level has her class elect offices periodically. Then, working with and through the officers, the teacher is able to have the students, take over such tasks as keeping the books in order or checking out playground equipment. One special merit that she sees in this plan is that it reduces the impression of "me *versus* them."

A secondary teacher arranged that members of his hobby club could work on a club project during their free time. Two boys had a fight in the club room. The teacher turned it over to the club members to decide the punishment that would be applied. They not only made the decision as to what should be done; they enforced their decision.

A teacher may encounter disappointments if he tries the approaches described above. However, some teachers seem to be able to get an excellent response using this system.

13. *Do not rush to give absolution.* According to the stimulus-response ideas of training, rewards or punishments should follow immediately after the act involved. However, this is not necessarily true in the discipline area. If the cycle of infraction-judgment-punishment moves rapidly, the offender can come out of it feeling that he now has a "clean slate." Many teachers find it best to move rather slowly in the process just described. A case that is in the pending category can give rise to a great deal of introspection and self-examination.

A certain junior high principal makes it a practice never to settle a major disciplinary problem on the day it arises. One reason is the danger that he might react with undue emotion. Another is that often after a cooling-off period, the attitude of the offender will have changed from hostility to some degree of cooperativeness.

IN CONCLUSION

Teachers cause discipline problems? It can happen. However, it sounds better if we state it in a positive sense. Good teachers periodically evaluate their own practices in terms of the effect on class discipline. An important guideline is: Make every effort to avoid a teacher-versus-class atmosphere.

Chapter 9
"If You Can't Control 'em, You Can't Learn 'em"
What Can Be Done?

Some of the points considered here might just as well be placed in one of the earlier chapters. Also, there will likely be some overlap between suggestions in this chapter and some that have already been discussed. Where this occurs, it is for the purpose of providing a proper emphasis on points of special importance.

1. *Know the law as it applies to disciplinary matters.* Since education is primarily a function of state and local government, the laws under which schools operate are mostly state and local laws. As a result, there is wide variation from one state to another. A secondary teacher had worked for a number of years in a state which permitted a teacher to use physical punishment. He moved to another state in which whipping was not legal. He started making free use of his belt only to find himself caught up in a major legal battle.

The laws do not vary just in terms of what the teacher can do; there is wide variability as to what the students can do. Some state laws spell out in considerable detail a code of student conduct, while in other states, very general terms are used. Information about such matters should be available to the teacher from the principal as well as from other sources.

2. *Know the local customs and conditions regarding discipline.* The laws just give part of the story. Local customs

can be very important. Two large high schools are part of the same system, and therefore operate under the same state and local regulations. In one school corporal punishment is forbidden, while in the other the principal makes frequent use of what he calls "the board of education." This difference in approach is strictly a matter of local custom. Knowledge about it is essential to the teachers involved.

Local conditions also can affect disciplinary measures. A new teacher told two junior high students that because of misbehavior, they would have to stay for thirty minutes after school. He did not realize that both boys rode a school bus and that they lived more than ten miles from the school. His effort to administer punishment was so unrealistic as to make him look quite foolish.

3. *Keep an eye on seating arrangements.* Sometimes students affect each other in ways that defy comprehension. Two students may be perfectly well behaved when apart but create problems when they are seated together. The logical solution is to keep them apart.

In many elementary classrooms, there is a great deal of movement, group work and constant rearrangement of furniture. Again, it is important that those students who catalyze each other in undesirable conduct be kept separated as much as possible. Have you ever noticed that this same phenomenon occurs among adults?

4. *Be sure that everyone has something to do.* The proverb "an idle mind is the devil's workshop" is still applicable. Nothing invites behavior problems more than to have blocks of time when nothing is expected of students.

A fourth grade teacher had a way of working with a few students at the board. During this time the other students were just in storage — no assignment, nothing expected of them. The result was pandemonium. Her supervisor suggested that the teacher assign material for the students to work on at their seats while she was at the board. The whole atmosphere changed as a result of this new approach.

Perhaps the concept described above needs a bit of qualifying. The students should have something to do *which they can handle.* The teacher who passes out too — difficult worksheets is merely adding a new dimension, frustration, to the list of problems.

Keeping the students busy at something they can do is doubly challenging in that they vary widely as to performance levels. Careful planning is necessary in order to meet the challenge, but many teachers meet it effectively.

5. *Vary the activities.* Much college teaching makes use of the lecture method. Since this is the procedure with which a young teacher has had recent contact, he or she might be inclined to rely on lecture, even with young children. With adults, lecture has many limitations, and this is doubly true of younger students.

We as teachers have to face the realities of limited attention span. Any type of teaching (not just lecture) must be restricted time-wise, depending on the age of the students. How do we know when it is time to change activities? The students tell us, through restlessness, misbehavior, lethargy and other such symptoms. The observant teacher comes to anticipate the need for change and avoids the problems.

In most situations, a drastic change is not required. A ninth grade science teacher had a practice of holding a class discussion of some sort, then terminating the hour with a study period. There were problems from two sources: (1) the discussion period was too long and (2) the students construed the end-of-the-hour study period as meaning the teacher had run out of something to do. She changed the schedule to put the block of time for study around the middle of the period. This gave the effect of three activities, discussion-study-discussion. Also, during the study block, the students had a specific assignment to work on, not a "do tomorrow's homework" kind of thing. This simple change in schedule greatly reduced the behavior problems associated with the earlier scheme.

6. *Think positively.* The story is told of two radio announcers whose ways of describing a particular day reflected their own personal outlooks. One said it was partly cloudy while the other said it was partly fair. So it is with teachers. One looks on Johnny's work in terms of "how far he has come" while the other thinks of "how far he has to go." Many students, especially those at lower performance levels, seldom hear an en-

couraging word regarding school work. Isn't it logical that many of them give up? This frequently leads to behavior problems.

This is not to say that the teacher must be the traditional pollyanna type of person. But if a student is given work at his "point of entry," then he is likely to succeed with it. This success should be properly recognized by the teacher, regardless of such considerations as grade level.

7. *Be a human being.* One critic has said that being a teacher seems, in some cases, to promote the development of a superman (or woman) complex. This criticism is hopefully invalid; yet there seems to be a fear, especially among young teachers, that their humanity might show through. A teacher who is relatively comfortable in a teaching situation does not hesitate to react in a human manner. This includes such traits as taking an interest in student activities, as well as in individual students; being aware of special problems in the life of the student; and having a sense of humor.

The sense of humor is of such importance that it is worthy of special attention. The teacher who can genuinely enjoy a laugh with students, and especially the teacher who can laugh at himself or herself, has a special advantage in averting certain types of disciplinary problems.

8. *Avoid group indictments.* A teacher can make himself look ridiculous if he is inclined to blast forth with a broadside of accusation because of misconduct on the part of a few students. A better strategy is to withhold comment until the source of the problem has been localized, then deal with the source.

A watch has been stolen in a home economics class, and considerable effort on the part of the teacher and principal had failed to locate it. The teacher in effect accused the entire class of the theft and added that nobody would leave her classroom until the watch was recovered. The latter was completely beyond her power to enforce and the broad-scale accusation only generated resentment against the teacher. When the watch was finally found, it developed that the thief was not a member of the class at all.

9. *Try to maintain good rapport with student leaders.* Naturally, we hope for good rapport with all students. But in

the area of keeping order, the leaders are especially important. Usually, even a casual observer can spot the leaders in a group. Some students will not follow such leaders but many will follow — laughing hilariously at the leader's not-very-funny remarks and in a variety of other ways. The teacher who can work on a constructive basis with these leaders has a big advantage.

An educator who works in a school for juvenile delinquents recently explained that he had little trouble as long as he was current regarding the "pecking order" among his students and has the leaders-of-the-moment working with him. His special problem was that, with a highly mobile student population, the leadership role was constantly changing.

10. *Avoid using school work for punishment.* Modern society, by law and/or by custom, circumscribes teachers as to how they may punish offenders. This has been discussed earlier. However, of all the means available, probably the least effective is the use of school work in a penal sense. The instantly-doubled assignment is the classic case. One authority has suggested that the reason many students dislike mathematics is that work in that area is often used for punishment. And the time-honored system of writing lines is a parallel system in language arts.

Is writing lines really punishment? One teacher assigned a middle elementary class the task of writing "I will come to class on time" 200 times. By stalling around, some students made this last all day — meanwhile avoiding doing other, more worthwhile work.

Sometimes tests are also used for punishment. This can only be classed as a mis-use of a valuable educational tool. Tests are seldom popular among students, even under the best conditions. Using tests for punishment merely adds to the problem.

11. *Keep referrals to a minimum.* A teacher who is confronted with a behavioral problem that is too serious for him or her to handle should enlist the help of the administration. But many teachers consider that a referral ("sending him to the office") is in some respects an admission of defeat. Such teachers exhaust all of the resources available to them before they make a referral.

Some principals find it hard to be patient with the teacher who makes constant referrals on the basis of petty infractions.

Yet such teachers consider even the most tactful suggestions that they handle such problems within the classroom as a lack of support from the administration. Such a situation can be minimized if the teacher will appeal for support only when the problem is clearly too big to be handled in the classroom.

12. *So far as possible, make corrections privately.* Sometimes behavioral problems arise which require that the teacher take prompt, vigorous action. But if the problem is not of an emergency nature, the better procedure is to discuss it with the student involved in a private setting. Let us consider the case of a real "wise guy." According to his set of values, he has won a victory if he can goad the teacher into a disciplinary scene in the presence of his peers. This serves to feed his ego and to make him a hero in the eyes of certain members of his class.

Many teachers have been surprised at the sort of person they encounter when they deal privately with the type of student described above. Without the moral support of his clique of fans, he may well be a frightened and insecure youngster who is hungry for adult attention and is willing to go to almost any lengths to get it.

13. *Learn as much as you can about the student.* A principal of a rural secondary school was a native of the community in which he worked. He was well informed as to the home background of practically all of his students. Newcomers to his faculty soon learned to consult the principal about problem students. Often he could provide information that was valuable to the teacher in dealing with the situation.

An integral part of problem solving, regardless of the nature of the problem, is to garner the necessary information. In dealing with a disciplinary case (a social problem), background information is vital. All sources — school records, the input of administrators, counselors and colleagues — have a contribution to make so that the teacher will not have to operate "in a vacuum" in dealing with a behavior problem.

14. *Work with parents as appropriate.* If we as teachers think students are confusing, we should consider the even higher level of confusion on the part of some parents, especially of those who lack the background to understand such phenomena as adolescence. However, in many situations, student behavior

problems are best dealt with when parents and the school officials are involved in a joint effort.

Some younger teachers dread the prospect of working with parents, the assumption being that it will be a *"me versus them"* situation. And indeed, it sometimes turns out that way. But in many cases, once communications are established, parents and teachers are mutually helpful in working on behavior problems.

In some school systems, there is a policy to the effect that all parent-teacher conferences are arranged by the central office, and frequently the principal or counselor participates. Before becoming involved in scheduling a meeting with parents, the teacher should find out how such matters are usually handled in the local situation. After all, as teachers we need all the help we can get!

15. *Don't look for the end of the list.* This story has no end. The list of suggestions regarding the teacher and class control could be continued almost indefinitely. However, many authorities in the area of student behavior feel that the points covered here have merit for the teacher as he or she deals with the vital area of class control. Why is this so important? "If you can't control 'em, you can't learn 'em."

IN CONCLUSION

What would you add to the list of 14 practices described in this chapter? Note that, once again, many of these suggestions are based on instruction, hence are within the purview of the teacher. Others emphasize knowledge — laws, customs, referral procedures, and others. If you should list these practices in order from most important to least important, which would head your list?

Suggested Readings

Adams, R., and Biddle, B. *Realities of teaching: Explorations with videotape.* New York: Holt, Rinehart and Winston, 1970.

Ahlstrom, W., and Havighurst, R. *400 losers.* San Francisco: Jossey-Boss, 1971.

Alexander, C., and Campbell, E. Peer influences on adolescent aspirations and attainments. *American Sociological Review,* 1964, *29,* 568-575.

Allen, K., Hart, B., Buell, J., Harris, F., and Wolf, M. Effects of social reinforcement on isolate behavior of a nursery school child. *Child Development,* 1964, *35,* 511-518.

Allen, K., Henke, L., Harris, F., Baer, D., and Reynolds, N. Control of hyperactivity by social reinforcement of attending behavior. *Journal of Educational Psychology,* 1967, *58,* 231-237.

Asher, S., and Markell, R. Sex differences in comprehension of high- and low-interest reading material. *Journal of Educational Psychology,* 1974, *66,* 680-687.

Aspy, D. Reaction to Carkhuff's articles. *Counseling Psychologist,* 1972, *3,* 35-41.

Aspy, D. The effect of teacher-offered conditions of empathy, congruence, and positive regard upon student achievement. *Florida Journal of Educational Research,* 1969, *11,* 39-48.

Aspy, D. and Buhler, J. The effect of teachers' inferred self-concept upon student achievement. *Journal of Educational Research,* 1975, *47,* 386-389.

Ausubel, D. *Educational psychology: A cognitive view.* New York: Holt, Rinehart and Winston, 1968.

Axline, V. *Play therapy.* Boston: Houghton Mifflin, 1947.

Bandura, A. *Principles of behavior modification.* New York: Holt, Rinehart, and Winston, 1969.

Barrish, H., Saunders, M., and Wolf, M. Good behavior game: Effects of individual contingencies for group consequences on disruptive behavior in a classroom. *Journal of Applied Behavior Analysis,* 1969, *2,* 119-124.

Bar-Tal, D., Bar-Tal, Y., and Leinhardt, G. *The environment, locus of control and feelings of satisfaction.* University of Pittsburgh, Learning and Research Development Center, 1975. (LRDC Publication 1975/27)

SUGGESTED READINGS

Bar-Tal, D., Bar-Zohar, Y. The relationship between perception of locus of control and academic achievement: Review and some educational implications. *Contemporary Educational Psychology,* 1977, *2,* 181-199.

Baumrind, D. Authoritarian vs. authoritative control. *Adolescence,* 1968, *3,* 255-272.

Becker, W., Engelmann, S., and Thomas, D. *Teaching 1: Classroom management.* Chicago: Research Press, 1975.

Becker, W. *Parents are teachers.* Champaign, Ill.: Research Press, 1971.

Becker, W., Madsen, C., Arnold, C., and Thomas, D. The contingent use of teacher attention and praise in reducing classroom behavior problems. *Journal of Special Education,* 1967, *1,* 287-307.

Beilin, H. The training and acquisition of logical operations. In M.F. Rosskopf, L.P. Steffe, and S. Taback (Eds.), *Piagetian Cognitive-Developmental Research and Mathematical Education.* Washington, D.C.: National Council of Teachers of Mathematics, 1971.

Belkin, G., and Gray, J. *Educational psychology: An introduction.* Dubuque, Iowa: Wm. C. Brown Company Publishers, 1977.

Bellack, A., Kiebard, H., Hyman, R., and Smith F. *The language of the classroom.* New York: Columbia University Teachers College Press, 1966.

Benedict, R. Continuities and discontinuities in cultural conditioning. In W. Martin and C. Stendler (Eds.), *Readings in Child Development.* New York: Harcourt Brace, 1954.

Berendal, R. *The influence of the group on the judgments of children.* New York: King's Crown Press, 1950.

Berenson, D. The effects of systematic human relations training upon the classroom performance of elementary school teachers. *Journal of Research Development in Education,* 1971, *4,* 70-85.

Bernard, H. *Child development and learning.* Boston: Allyn and Bacon, 1973.

Bissell, J., White, S., and Zivin, G. Sensory modalities in children's learning. In G.S. Lesser (Ed.), *Psychology and educational practice.* Glenview, Ill.: Scott, Foresman, 1971.

Blackman, G., and Silberman, A. *Modification of child and adolescent behavior.* Belmont, Calif.: Wadsworth, 1975.

Blair, J. The effects of differential reinforcement on the discrimination learning of normal and low-achieving middle-class boys. *Child Development,* 1972, *43,* 251-255.

Bloom, B. (Ed.). *Taxonomy of educational objectives, handbook I: Cognitive domain.* New York: David McKay, 1956.

Bolles, R. Reinforcement, expectancy, and learning. *Psychological Review,* 1972, *79,* 394-409.

Bolstad, O., and Johnson, S. Self-regulation in the modification of disruptive classroom behavior. *Journal of Applied Behavior Analysis,* 1972, *5,* 433-454.

Brainerd, C., and Allen, T. Experimental inductions of the conservation of 'first order' quantitative invariants. *Psychological Bulletin,* 1971, *75,* 128-144.

Branch, C., Damico, S., and Purkey, W. A comparison between the self-concepts as learner of disruptive and nondisruptive middle school students. *The Middle School Journal,* 1977, *7,* 15-16.

Brittain, C. Age and sex of siblings and conformity toward parents versus peers in adolescence. *Child Development,* 1966, *37,* 709-714.

Brittain, C. Adolescent choices and parent-peer cross-pressures. *American Sociological Review,* 1963, *28,* 385-390.

Broden, M., Hall, R., Dunlap, A., and Clark, R. Effects of teacher attention and a token reinforcement system in a junior high school special education class. *Exceptional Children,* 1970, *36,* 341-349.

Broden, M., Hall, R., and Mitts, B. The effect of self-recording on the classroom behavior of two eighth-grade students. *Journal of Applied Behavior Analysis,* 1971, *4,* 191-199.

Bronfenbrenner, U. Disturbing changes in the American family. *Education Digest,* 1977a, *42,* 22-25.

Bronfenbrenner, U. Nobody home: The erosion of the American family. *Psychology Today,* May, 1977b, *10,* 40-47.

Bronfenbrenner, U. The origins of alienation. *Scientific American,* 1974, *231,* 53-57.

Bronfenbrenner, U. *Two worlds of childhood: U.S. and U.S.S.R.* New York: Russell Sage Foundation, 1970.

Brookover, W., Patterson, A., and Thomas, S. *Self-concept of ability and school achievement.* U.S. Office of Education, Cooperative Research Project No. 845. East Lansing: Office of Research and Publication. Michigan State University, 1965.

Brophy, J., and Evertson, C. *Learning from teaching: A developmental perspective.* Boston: Allyn and Bacon, 1976.

Brophy, J., and Good, T. *Teacher-student relationships: Causes and consequences.* New York: Holt, Rinehart, and Winston, 1974.

Brophy, J., and Good, T. Teacher's communication on differential expectations for children's classroom performance: Some behavioral data. *Journal of Educational Psychology,* 1971, *61,* 365-374.

Brown, E., and Shields, E. Results with systematic suspension: A guidance technique to help children develop self-control in public school classrooms. *Journal of Special Education,* 1967, *1,* 425-437.

Brown, G. The training of teachers for affective roles. In K. Ryan (Ed.), *The Seventy-Fourth Yearbook of the National Society for the Study of Education.* Chicago: University of Chicago Press, 1975.

Brunkan, R., and Sheni, F. Personality characteristics of ineffective, effective and efficient readers. *Personnel and Guidance Journal,* 1966, *44,* 837-844.

Bryan, J., and Locke, E. Goal setting as a means of increasing motivation. *Journal of Applied Psychology,* 1967, *51,* 274-277.

Burrows, C. The effects of a mastery learning strategy on the geometry achievement of fourth and fifth grade children. Unpublished doctoral dissertation, Indiana University, 1973.

Campbell, P. School and self concept. *Educational Leadership,* 1967, *24,* 510-515.

Carkhuff, R. *Helping and human relations: A primer for lay and professional helpers. Vol. 2: Practice and research.* New York: Holt, Rinehart and Winston, 1969.

Carrino, C. Identifying potential dropouts in the elementary grades. *Dissertation Abstracts,* 1966, *27,* 343.

SUGGESTED READINGS

Casler, L. The effects of extra tactile stimulation on a group of institutionalized infants. *Genetic Psychology Monographs,* 1965, *71,* 137-175.

Castillo, G. *Left-handed teaching: Lessons in affective education.* New York: Praeger Publishers, 1974.

Chaikin, A., Sigler, E., and Derlega, V. Nonverbal mediators of teacher expectancy effects. *Journal of Personality and Social Psychology,* 1974, *30,* 144-149.

Chandler, T. Locus of control: A proposal for change. *Psychology in the Schools,* 1975, *12,* 334-339.

Coats, W., and Smidchens, U. Audience recall as a function of speaker dynamism. *Journal of Educational Psychology,* 1966, *57,* 189-191.

Coleman, J. *Equality of educational opportunity.* Washington, D.C.: U.S. Department of Health, Education, and Welfare, Office of Education, 1966.

Collins, K. A strategy for mastery learning in modern mathematics. In J. Block (Ed.), *Mastery Learning: Theory and Practice.* New York: Holt, Rinehart and Winston, 1971.

Combs, A., Avila, D., and Purkey, W. *Helping relationships: Basic concepts for the helping professions.* Boston: Allyn and Bacon, 1971.

Combs, A., and Taylor, C. The effect of the perception of mild degrees of threat on performance. *Journal of Abnormal and Social Psychology,* 1952, *47,* 420-424.

Conger, J. *Adolescence and youth: Psychological development in a changing world.* New York: Harper and Row, 1977.

Conger, J., Miller, W., and Walsmith, C. Antecedents of delinquency, personality, social class and intelligence. In P. Mussen, J. Conger, and J. Kagen (Eds.), *Readings in Child Development and Personality.* New York: Harper and Row, 1965.

Coopersmith, S. *The antecedents of self-esteem.* San Francisco: W.H. Freeman, 1967.

Copeland, R., Brown, R., and Hall, R. The effects of principal-implemented techniques on the behavior of pupils. *Journal of Applied Behavior Analysis,* 1974, *7,* 77-86.

Cormany, R. *Guidance and counseling in Pennsylvania: Status and needs.* Lemoyne, Pa.: ESEA Title III Project, West Shore School District, 1975.

Costello, C. Ego-involvement, success and failure: A review of the literature. In H.J. Eysenck (Ed.), *Experiments in motivation.* New York: Macmillan, 1964.

Covington, M., and Beery, R. *Self-worth and school learning.* New York: Holt, Rinehart and Winston, 1976.

Craighead, W., Kazdin, A., and Mahoney, M. *Behavior modification: Principles, issues, and applications.* Boston: Houghton Mifflin, 1976.

Curwin, R., and Fuhrmann, B. *Discovering your teaching self: Humanistic approaches to effective teaching.* Englewood Cliffs, N.J., 1975.

Daum, J. Proxemics in the classroom: Speaker-subject distance and educational performance. Paper presented at the annual meeting of the Southeastern Psychological Association, 1972.

Davidson, H., and Lang, G. Children's perceptions of their teachers' feelings toward them. *Journal of Experimental Education,* 1960, *29,* 109-118.

Davis, J., Laughlin, P., and Komorita, S. The social psychology of small groups: Cooperative and mixed-motive interaction. In M. Rosenzweig and L. Porter (Eds.) *Annual Review of Psychology.* Palo Alto, California: Annual Reviews Inc., 1976, *27,* 501-542.

DeCharms, R. *Enhancing motivation.* New York: Irvington Publishers, 1976.

DeCharms, R. Personal causation training in schools. *Journal of Applied Social Psychology,* 1972, *2,* 95-113.

DeCharms, R. From pawns to origins: Toward self-motivation. In G.S. Lesser (Ed.) *Psychology and educational practice.* Glenview, Ill: Scott Foresman, 1971.

DeCharms, R. *Personal causation.* New York: Academic Press, 1968.

Deci, E. The effects of contingent and noncontingent rewards and controls on intrinsic motivation. *Organizational Behavior and Human Performance,* 1972, *8,* 217-229.

Deci, E. Effects of externally mediated rewards on intrinsic motivation. *Journal of Personality and Social Psychology,* 1971, *18,* 105-115.

deHirsch, K., Jansky, J., and Langford, W. *Predicting reading failure.* New York: Harper and Row, 1966.

Delefes, P., and Jackson, B. Teacher-pupil interaction as a function of location in the classroom. *Psychology in the School,* 1972, *9,* 119-123.

Dembo, M. *Teaching for learning: Applying educational psychology in the classroom.* Santa Monica, Calif.: Goodyear, 1977.

Dennis, W. Causes of retardation among institutional children: Iran. *Journal of Genetic Psychology,* 1960, *96,* 46-60.

DeVries, D. and Edwards, K. Learning games and student teams: Their effects on classroom process. *American Educational Research Journal,* 1973, *10,* 307-318.

Dewey, J. *Experience and education.* New York: The Macmillan Co., 1963.

Dewey, J. *Experience and nature.* LaSalle, Illinois: The Open Court Publishing Company, 1958.

Diggory, J. *Self-evaluation: Concepts and studies.* New York: John Wiley and Sons, 1966.

Dooling, D., and Mullet, R. Locus of thematic effects in retention of prose. *Journal of Experimental Psychology,* 1973, *97,* 404-406.

Drabman, R., and Lahey, B. Feedback in classroom behavior modification: Effects on the target child and her classmates. *Journal of Applied Behavior Analysis,* 1974, *7,* 591-598.

Drabman, R., Spitalnik, R., and O'Leary, K. Teaching self-control to disruptive children. *Journal of Abnormal Psychology,* 1973, *82,* 10-16.

Dreikurs, R. *Psychology in the classroom: A manual for teachers,* 2nd ed. New York: Harper and Row, 1968.

Dreikurs, R., and Cassel, P. *Discipline without tears: What to do with children who misbehave,* New York: Hawthorn Books, 1972.

Dreikurs, R., Grunwald, B., and Pepper, F. *Maintaining sanity in the classroom: Illustrated teaching techniques.* New York: Harper and Row, 1971.

Duckworth, E. Piaget rediscovered. In R.E. Ripple and V.N. Rockcastle (Eds.), *Piaget rediscovered: A report of the conference on cognitive skills and curriculum development.* Ithaca, N.Y.: Cornell University, School of Education, 1964.

SUGGESTED READINGS

Duke, D. How administrators view the crisis in school discipline. *Phi Delta Kappan,* 1978, *59,* 325-330.

Dunn, R., and Dunn, K. Learning styles/teaching styles: Should they . . . can they . . . be matched? *The Journal of Educational Leaderships,* 1979, *36,* 238-244.

Dunn, R., and Dunn, K. *Teaching students through their individual learning styles: A practical approach.* Reston, Virginia: Reston Publishing Co., Division of Prentice-Hall, Inc., 1978.

Dunn, R., and Dunn, K. *Practical approaches to individualizing instruction: Contracts and other effective teaching strategies.* West Nyack, New York: Parker Publishing Co., Inc., 1972.

Dunn, R., and Goldman, M. Competition and noncompetition in relationship to satisfaction and feelings toward own group and nongroup members. *Journal of Social Psychology,* 1966, *68,* 299-311.

Elder, G. Parental power legitimation and its effect on the adolescent. *Sociometry,* 1963, *26,* 50-65.

Elkind, D. Growing up faster. *Psychology Today,* 1979, *12,* 38-45.

Epstein, M., Hallahan, D., and Kauffman, J. Implications of the reflectivity-impulsivity dimension for special education. *Journal of Special Education,* 1975, *9,* 11-25.

Erikson, E. *Identity, youth, and crisis.* New York: W.W. Norton & Co., 1968.

Erikson, E. *Childhood and society* (2nd ed.). New York: Norton, 1963.

Faris, R. High and low achievement of intellectually average intermediate grade students related to the self concept and social approval. *Dissertation Abstracts,* 1967, *28,* 1205.

Farquhar, W. *A comprehensive study of the motivational factors underlying achievement of eleventh-grade high-school students.* U.S. Office of Education, Cooperative Research Report No. 846. East Lansing: Office of Research and Publications, Michigan State University, 1968.

Federal Bureau of Investigations, U.S. Department of Justice. *Uniform crime reports.* Washington, D.C.: U.S. Government Printing Office, 1975.

Fernandez, C., Espinosa, R., and Dornbusch, S. Discussed in Martin, D. Your praise can smother learning. *Learning,* 1977, *5,* 43-51.

Fisher, B., and Fisher, L. Styles in teaching and learning. *The Journal of Educational Leadership,* 1979, *36,* 245-254.

Flanders, N. *Analyzing teaching behavior.* Reading, Mass.: Addison-Wesley, 1970.

Flanders, N. Intent, action and feedback: A preparation for teaching. *The Journal of Teacher Education,* 1963, *14,* 251-260.

Flanders, N., and Amidon, E. *The role of the teacher in the classroom.* Minneapolis, Minn.: Minneapolis Association for Productive Teaching, 1967.

Flanders, N., Morrison, B., and Brode, E. Changes in pupil attitudes during the school year. *Journal of Educational Psychology,* 1968, *59,* 334-338.

Fredericks, B. *Personal communications.* Unpublished Research Project, Teaching Research, Monmouth, Oregon, 1975.

Fredericks, B., Baldwin, V., Moore, W., McDonnell, J., Dalke, B., and Moore, M. Impact 6 of the Title VI Programs in Oregon, September 1971-August 1972. Monmouth, Oregon: Teaching Research, 1972.

Friedrich, L., and Stein, A. Aggressive and prosocial TV programs and the natural behavior of preschool children. *Monographs of the Society for Research in Child Development,* 1973, *38,* (4, Serial No. 151).

Gallagher, J. Expressive thought by gifted children in the classroom. *Elementary English,* 1965, *42,* 559-568.

Gibb, J. *Climate for trust formation.* In L. Bradford, J. Gibb, and K. Beene (Eds.), *T-Group Theory and Laboratory Method.* New York: John Wiley and Sons, 1964, 279-309.

Ginott, H. *Between parent and child: New solutions to old problems.* New York: Macmillan, 1965.

Glasser, W. *Schools without failure.* New York: Harper and Row, 1969.

Glasser, W. *Reality therapy.* New York: Harper and Row, 1965.

Goertzel, V., and Goertzel, M. *Cradles of eminance.* Boston: Little, Brown, 1962.

Good, T., and Brophy, J. *Looking in classrooms.* New York: Harper and Row, 1973.

Good, T. Which pupils do you call on? *The Elementary School Journal,* 1970, *10,* 190-198.

Goodwin, S., and Mahoney, M. Modification of aggression through modeling: An experimental probe. *Journal of Behavior Therapy and Experimental Psychiatry,* 1975, *6,* 200-202.

Gordon, I. *Studying the child in school.* New York, Wiley, 1966.

Gordon, T. *Parent effectiveness training: The tested new way to raise responsible children.* New York: Wyden, 1970.

Gordon, T. *Teacher Effectiveness Training.* New York: Wyden, 1974.

Gordon T., and Breivogel, W. *Building effective home-school relationships.* Boston: Allyn and Bacon, 1976.

Gowan, J. Factors of achievement in high school and college. *Journal of Counseling Psychology,* 1960, *7,* 91-95.

Gray, R., Graubard, P., and Rosenberg, H. Little brother is changing you. *Psychology Today,* November, 1974, *7,* 42-46.

Greenwood, C., and Hops, H. Generalization of teacher praising skills over time and setting: What you teach is what you get. Paper presented at the 54th Annual Convention of the Council for Exceptional Children, Chicago, Ill., 1976.

Greenwood, C., Hops, H., Delquadri, J., and Walker, H. *PASS: Program for academic survival skills.* Eugene, Oregon: Center at Oregon for Research in the Behavioral Education of the Handicapped, 1974.

Grimes, J., and Allinsmith, W. Compulsivity, anxiety, and school achievement. *Merrill-Palmer Quarterly,* 1961, *7,* 247-272.

Hagen, J., and Hale, G. The development of attention in children. In A.D. Pick (Ed.), *Minnesota Symposis on Child Psychology (Vol. 7).* Minneapolis: University of Minnesota Press, 1972.

Hall, R., Lund, D., and Jackson, D. Effects of teacher attention on study behavior. *Journal of Applied Behavior Analysis,* 1968, *1,* 1-12.

Hargreaves, D. *Social relations in a secondary school.* Atlantic Highlands, New Jersey: Humanities Press, 1967.

Harlow, H. The nature of love. *American Psychologist,* 1958, *13,* 673-684.

Harmin, M., Kirschenbaum, H., and Simon, S. *Clarifying values through subject matter.* Minneapolis, Minn.: Winston Press, 1973.

SUGGESTED READINGS

Hawley, R., and Hawley, I. *Human values in the classroom: A handbook for teachers.* New York: Hart Publishing Co., 1975.

Hefele, T. The effects of systematic human relations training upon student achievement. *Journal of Research and Development in Education,* 1971, *4,* 52-69.

Henry, J. *Culture against man.* New York: Random House, 1963.

Hewett, F. *Education of exceptional learners.* Boston: Allyn and Bacon, 1974.

Holmes, D., and Barthell, C. High school yearbooks: A nonreactive measure of social isolation in graduates who later become schizophrenic. *Journal of Abnormal Psychology,* 1968, *73,* 313-316.

Holt, J. *What do I do Monday?* New York: Dell Publishing Co., 1972.

Holt, J. *The underachieving school.* New York: Pitman, 1969.

Holzman, P., and Grinker, R. Schizophrenia in adolescence. In S. Feinstein and P. Giovacchini (Eds.), *Adolescent Psychiatry Volume V.* New York: Jason Aronson, Inc., 1977.

Hudgins, B., and Ahlbrand, W., Jr. A study of classroom interaction and thinking. Technical report series No. 8. St. Ann, MO: Central Midwestern Regional Educational Laboratory, 1969.

Hughes, E., Becker, H., and Greer, B. Student culture and academic effort. In N. Sanford (Ed.) *The American College.* New York: Wiley and Sons, 1962.

Hundert, J. The effectiveness of reinforcement, response cost, and mixed programs on classroom behaviors. *Journal of Applied Behavior Analysis,* 1976, *9,* 107.

Hutzell, R., Platzek, D., and Logue, P. Control of symptoms of Gilles de la Tourette's Syndrome by self-monitoring. *Journal of Behavior Therapy and Experimental Psychiatry,* 1974, *5,* 71-76.

Ince, L. The use of relaxation training and a conditioned stimulus in the elimination of epileptic seizures in a child: A case study. *Journal of Behavior Therapy and Experimental Psychiatry,* 1976, *7,* 39-42.

Irwin, F. Sentence completion responses and scholastic success or failure. *Journal of Counseling Psychology,* 1967, *14,* 269-271.

Jackson, P. *Life in classrooms.* New York: Holt, Rinehart and Winston, 1968.

Jacobs, J. *Adolescent suicide.* New York: Wiley, 1971.

Jacobson, E. *Progressive relaxation.* Chicago: University of Chicago Press, 1938.

Johnson, D. *Educational Psychology.* Englewood Cliffs, N.J.: Prentice-Hall, 1979.

Johnson, D., and Johnson, R. (Eds.) Social interdependence in the classroom: Cooperation, competition and individualism; symposium. *Journal of Research and Development in Education,* 1978, *12,* 1-152.

Johnson, D., and Johnson, R. *Learning together and alone: Cooperation, competition and individualization.* Englewood Cliffs, N.J.: Prentice-Hall, 1975a.

Johnson, D., and Johnson, F. *Joining together: Group theory and group skills.* Englewood Cliffs, N.J.: Prentice-Hall, 1975b.

Johnson, S. Self-reinforcement versus external reinforcement in behavior modification with children. *Developmental Psychology,* 1970, *3,* 147-148.

Johnson, S., and Martin, S. Developing self-evaluation as a conditioned reinforcer. In B. Ashem and E. Poser (Eds.) *Behavior Modification With Children.* New York: Pergamon, 1973, 69-78.

Jones, V. *Adolescents with behavior problems: Strategies for teaching, counseling, and parent involvement.* Boston: Allyn and Bacon, 1980.

Jones, V. A junior high school program for emotionally disturbed children. In J. McDonnel, H. Fredericks, V. Baldwin, W. Moore, R. Crowley, R. Anderson, and K. Moore (Eds.) *Impact 7 of the Title VI Programs in the State of Oregon, September 1972-August 1973.* Monmouth, Oregon: Teaching Research, 1973.

Jones, V. A junior high school program for emotionally disturbed children. In H. Fredericks, V. Baldwin, W. Moore, J. McDonnel, B. Dalke, and M. Moore (Eds.) *Impact 6 of the Title VI Programs in the State of Oregon,* September 1971-August 1972. Monmouth, Oregon: Teaching Research, 1972.

Jones, V. The influence of teacher-student introversion, achievement, and similarity on teacher-student dyadic classroom interactions. *Dissertation Abstracts,* 1972, 6205-6206A.

Kagan, J. Reflection-impulsivity. *Journal of Abnormal Psychology,* 1966, *71,* 17-24.

Kagan, J., Moss, H., and Siegel, I. Psychological significance of styles of conceptualization. In J.C. Wright and J. Kagan (Eds.), Basic cognitive processes in children. *Monographs of the Society for Research in Child Development,* 1963, *28,* 260.

Kamii, C. *An application of Piaget's theory to the conceptualization of a preschool curriculum.* In R.K. Parker (Ed.), *The Preschool in Action.* Boston: Allyn and Bacon, 1972.

Kazdin, A. The effect of vicarious reinforcement on attentive behavior in the classroom. *Journal of Applied Behavior Analysis,* 1973, *6,* 71-78.

Kazdin, A. Response cost: The removal of conditioned reinforcers for therapeutic change. *Behavior Therapy,* 1972, *3,* 533-546.

Kazdin, A., and Bootzin, R. The token economy: An evaluative review. *Journal of Applied Behavior Analysis,* 1972, *5,* 343-372.

Kazdin, A., and Kpock, J. The effect of nonverbal teacher approval on student attentive behavior. *Journal of Applied Behavior Analysis,* 1973, *6,* 643-654.

Keirsey, D. Systematic exclusion: Eliminating chronic classroom disruptions. In J. Krumboltz and C. Thoresen (Eds.), *Behavioral counseling: Case studies and techniques.* New York: Holt, Rinehart and Winston, 1969, 89-113.

Kennedy, B. Motivational effect of individual conferences and goal setting on performance and attitudes in arithmetic. ERIC: ED 032113, 1968.

Klein, R., and Schuler, C. Increasing academic performance through the contingent use of self-evaluation. Paper presented at the Annual Meeting of the American Educational Research Association, Chicago, April, 1974.

Kleinfeld, J. Effective teachers of Indian and Eskimo students. *School Review,* 1975, *83,* 301-344.

Kleinfeld, J. *Instructional style and the intellectual performance of Indian and Eskimo students.* Final Report, Project No. 1-J-027, Office of Education, U.S. Department of Health, Education and Welfare, 1972.

SUGGESTED READINGS

Knaus, W. *Rational-emotive education: A manual for elementary school teachers.* New York: Institute for Rational Living, 1974.

Kohl, H. *36 children.* New York: New American Library, 1967.

Kohlberg, L. Development of moral character and moral ideology. In J.L. Hoffman and L.W. Hoffman (Eds.) *Review of Child Development Research.* New York: Russell Sage Foundation, 1964.

Kohlberg, L. Moral stages and moralization. The cognitive-developmental approach. In T. Lickona (Ed.), *Moral Development and Behavior.* New York: Holt, Rinehart and Winston, 1976.

Kounin, J. *Discipline and group management in classrooms.* New York: Holt, Rinehart and Winston, 1970.

Kranzler, G. *You can change the way you feel: A rational-emotive approach.* Eugene, Oregon: Published by author, Counseling Department, University of Oregon, 1974.

Krathwohl, D., Bloom, B., and Masia, B. *Taxonomy of educational objectives, handbook II: Affective domain.* New York: David McKay, 1964.

LaBenne, W., and Greene, B. *Educational implications of self-concept theory.* Pacific Palisades, Calif.: Goodyear, 1969.

Landry, R. Achievement and self concept: A curvilinear relationship. Paper presented at American Educational Research Association Convention, Chicago, 1974.

Landry, R., and Edeburn, C. Teacher self-concept and student self-concept. Paper presented at American Educational Research Association Convention, Chicago, 1974.

Leonard, G. *Education and ecstasy.* New York: Dell, 1968.

Lepper, M., and Greene, D. Turning play into work: Effects of adult surveillance and extrinsic rewards on children's intrinsic motivation. *Journal of Personality and Social Psychology,* 1975, *31,* 479-486.

Levin, G., and Simmons, J. Response to food and praise by emotionally disturbed boys. *Psychological Reports,* 1962, *11,* 539-546.

Lewis, R., and St. John, N. Contribution of cross-racial friendship to minority group achievement in desegregated classrooms. *Sociometry,* 1974, *37,* 79-91.

Lorber, N. Inadequate social acceptance and disruptive classroom behavior. *Journal of Educational Research,* 1966, *59,* 360-362.

Lovitt, T., and Curtiss, K. Effects of manipulating an antecedent event on mathmatics response rate. *Journal of Applied Behavior Analysis,* 1968, *1,* 329-333.

Madsen, C., Becker, W., and Thomas, D. Rules, praise, and ignoring: Elements of elementary classroom control. *Journal of Applied Behavior Analysis,* 1968, *1,* 139-150.

Madsen, C., Madsen, C., Saudargus, R., Hammond, W., and Edgar, D. Classroom RAID (Rules, Approval, Ignore, Disapproval): A cooperative approach for professionals and volunteers. Unpublished manuscript, University of Florida, 1970.

Maehr, M. Continuing motivation: An analysis of a seldom considered educational outcome. *Review of Educational Research,* 1976, *46,* 443-462.

Maehr, M. *Sociocultural origins of achievement.* Monterey, Calif.: Brooks/Cole, 1974.

Maehr, M., and Sjogren, D. Atkinson's theory of achievement motivation: First step toward a theory of academic motivation. *Review of Educational Research,* 1971, *41,* 143-161.

Mahoney, M. *Cognition and behavior modification.* Cambridge, Mass.: Ballinger, 1974.

Mannheim, B. An investigation of the interrelations of reference groups, membership groups and the self-image: A test of the Cooley-Mead Theory of the self. *Dissertation Abstracts,* 1957, *17,* 1616-1617.

Maslow, A. *Toward a psychology of being.* New York: D. Van Nostrand, 1968.

Mason, W. Determinants of social behavior in young chimpanzees. In A.M. Schrier, H.F. Harlow, and F. Stolenits (Eds.), *Behavior of Non-Human Primates,* Vol. 2, New York: Academic Press, 1965, 287-334.

McClelland, D., and Alschuler, A. The achievement motivation development project. Final report to USOE project No. 7-1231, Bureau of Research, 1971.

McClelland, D., Atkinson, J., Clark, R., and Lowell, E. *The achievement motive.* New York: Appleton-Century-Crofts, 1953.

McGinley, P., and McGinley. Reading groups as psychological groups. *Journal of Experimental Education,* 1970, *39,* 35-42.

McKenzie, H., Clark, M., Wolf, M., Kothera, R., and Benson, C. Behavior modification of children with learning disabilities using grades as tokens and allowances as back-up reinforcers. *Exceptional Children,* 1968, *34,* 745-752.

McKenzie, T., and Rushall, B. Effects of self-recording on attendance and performance in a competitive swimming training program. *Journal of Applied Behavior Analysis,* 1974, *7,* 199-206.

McLaughlin, T., and Malaby, J. Reducing and measuring inappropriate verbalizations in a token classroom. *Journal of Applied Behavior Analysis,* 1972, *5,* 329-333.

Mead, M. *Culture and commitment: A study of the generation gap.* Garden City, NY: Doubleday, 1970.

Medley, D. *Teacher competence and teacher effectiveness, a review of process-product research August, 1977.* American Association of Colleges for Teacher Education. Education. Washington, D.C., August, 1977.

Meichenbaum, D., and Cameron, R. The clinical potential of modifying what clients say to themselves. In M. Mahoney and C. Thoresen (Eds.) *Self-control: Power to the person.* Monterey, Calif.: Brooks/Cole, 1974, 263-290.

Messick, S. The criterion problem in the evaluation of instruction. In M.C. Wittrock and D.E. Wiley (Eds.), *The evaluation of instruction: Issues and problems.* New York: Holt, Rinehart and Winston, 1970.

Meunier, C., and Rule, B. Anxiety, confidence and conformity. *Journal of Personality,* 1967, *35,* 498-504.

Middleton, R., and Snell, P. Political expression of adolescent rebellion. *American Journal of Sociology,* 1963, *68,* 527-535.

Monohan, J., and O'Leary, K. Effects of self-instruction on rule-breaking behavior. *Psychological Reports,* 1971, *29,* 1059-1066.

Mordock, J. *The other child: An introduction to exceptionality.* New York: Harper, 1975.

SUGGESTED READINGS

Morris, J. *Psychology and teaching: A humanistic view.* New York: Random House, 1978.

Morrison, A., and McIntyre, D. *Teachers and teaching.* Baltimore: Penguin Books, 1969.

Morse, W. Self-concept in the school setting. *Childhood Education,* 1964, *41,* 195-198.

Muldoon, J. The concentration of liked and disliked members in groups and the relationship of the concentration to group cohesiveness. *Sociometry,* 1955, *18,* 73-81.

Muuss, R. *Theories of adolescence* (3rd ed.). New York: Random House, 1975.

O'Leary, K., and Becker, W. Behavior modification of an adjustment class: A token reinforcement program. *Exceptional Children,* 1967, *33,* 637-642.

O'Leary, K., Becker, W., Evans, M., and Saudergas, R. A token reinforcement program in a public school: A replication and systematic analysis. *Journal of Applied Behavior Analysis,* 1969, *2,* 3-13.

O'Leary, K., and Drabman, R. Token reinforcement programs in the classroom. A review. *Psychological Bulletin,* 1971, *75,* 379-398.

Packard, R. The control of classroom attention: A group contingency for complex behavior. *Journal of Applied Behavior Analysis,* 1970, *3,* 13-28.

Page, E. Teacher comments and student performance. *Journal of Educational Psychology,* 1958, *49,* 172-181.

Patterson, C. *Humanistic education.* Englewood Cliffs, N.J.: Prentice-Hall, 1973.

Patterson, G. *Families: Applications of social learning to family life.* Champaign, Ill.: Research Press, 1971.

Patterson, G. Behavioral intervention procedures in the classroom and in the home. In A.E. Berzin and S.L. Garfield (Eds.), *Handbook of psychotherapy and behaviour change: An empirical analysis.* New York: Wiley, 1971.

Patterson, G. *Living with children: New methods for parents and teachers.* Champaign, Ill.: Research Press, 1968.

Perline, I., and Levinsky, D. Controlling behavior in the severely retarded. *American Journal of Mental Deficiency,* 1968, *73,* 74-78.

Piaget, J. The role of action in the development of thinking. In W.F. Overton and J.M. Gallagher (Eds.), *Knowledge and Development (Vol. 1).* New York: Plenum, 1977.

Piaget, J. Piaget's theory. In P.H. Mussen (Ed.), *Carmichael's Manual of Child Psychology* (3rd ed., Vol. 1). New York: Wiley, 1970.

Piaget, J. *The origins of intelligence in children* (M. Cook, Trans.). New York: International Universities Press, 1952.

Phillips, E. Achievement place: Token reinforcement procedures in a home-style rehabilitation setting for "pre-delinquent" boys. *Journal of Applied Behavior Analysis,* 1968, *1,* 213-224.

Purkey, W. *Inviting school success: A self-concept approach to teaching and learning.* Belmont, Calif.: Wadsworth, 1978.

Purkey, W. *Self-concept and school achievement.* Englewood Cliffs, N.J.: Prentice-Hall, 1970.

Putney, S., and Putney, G. *The adjusted American: Normal neurosis in American society.* New York: Harper and Row, 1964.

Ramirez, M., and Castaneda, A. *Cultural democracy, bicognitive development, and education.* New York: Academic Press, 1974.

Reckinger, N. Choice as a way to quality learning. *The Journal of Educational Leadership,* 1979, *36,* 255-256.

Reese, H. Relationships between self-acceptance and sociometric choices. *Journal of Abnormal and Social Psychology,* 1961, *62,* 472-474.

Reissman, F. The strategy of style. *Teachers College Record,* 1964, *65,* 484-495.

Rist, R. Student social class and teacher expectations: The self-fulling prophecy in ghetto educaiton. *Harvard Educational Review,* 1970, *40,* 411-451.

Robert, Marc. *School morale: The human dimension.* Niles, Illinois: Argus Communications, 1976.

Rogers, C. The characteristics of a helping relationship. *Personnel and Guidance Journal,* 1958, *37,* 6-16.

Rogers, C. *Freedom to learn.* Columbus, Ohio: Charles E. Merrill, 1969.

Rosenkrantz, A. A note on adolescent suicide: Incidence, dynamics, and some suggestions for treatment. *Adolescence,* 1978, *13,* 209-214.

Rosenshine, B. Classroom instruction. In N. Gage (Ed.), *The psychology of teaching methods.* National Society for the Study of Education Seventy-Seventh Yearbook, 1976.

Rosenshine, B. Enthusiastic teaching: a research review. *School Review,* 1970, *72,* 499-514.

Rosenshine, B., and Furst, N. The use of direct observation to study teaching. In R. Travers (Ed.), *Second handbook of research on teaching.* Chicago: Rand McNally, 1973.

Rosenthal, R. The pygmalion effect lives. *Psychology Today,* 1973, *7,* 56-63.

Rosenthal, R., and Jacobson, L. *Pygmalion in the classroom: Teacher expectation and pupils intellectual development.* New York: Holt, Rinehart and Winston, 1968.

Rotter, J. Generalized expectancies for internal versus external control of reinforcement. *Psychological Monographs,* 1966, 80.

Rotter, J. *Social learning and clinical psychology.* Englewood Cliffs, N.J.: Prentice-Hall, 1954.

Rowe, M. Wait-time and rewards as instructional variables, their influence on language, logic, and fate control: Part one, wait-time. *Journal of Research in Science Teaching,* 1974, *11,* 81-94.

Runkel, P., Lawrence, M., Oldfield, S., Rider, M., and Clark, C. Stages of group development: An empirical test of Tuckman's hypothesis. *Journal of Applied Behavioral Science,* 1971, *7,* 180-193.

Schmidt, G., and Ulrich, R. Effects of group contingent events upon classroom noise. *Journal of Applied Behavior Analysis,* 1969, *2,* 171-179.

Schmuck, R. Some aspects of classroom social climate. *Psychology in the Schools,* 1966, *3,* 59-65.

Schmuck, R. Some relationships of peer liking patterns in the classroom to pupil attitudes and achievement. *School Review,* 1963, *71,* 337-359.

Schmuck, R., and Schmuck, R. *Group processes in the classroom.* Dubuque, Iowa: Wm. C. Brown, 1975.

SUGGESTED READINGS

Schmuck, R., and Schmuck, P. *A humanistic psychology of education: Making the school everybody's house.* Palo Alto, Calif.: National Press Books, 1974.

Schutz, W. *The interpersonal underworld.* Palo Alto, Calif.: Science and Behavior Books, 1966.

Schwebel, A., and Cherlin, D. Physical and social distancing in teacher-pupil relationships. *Journal of Educational Psychology,* 1972, *63,* 543-550.

Sebald, H. *Adolesence: A social psychological analysis.* Englewood Cliffs, N.J.: Prentice-Hall, 1977.

Sgan, M. Social reinforcement, socioeconomic status, and susceptibility to experimenter influence. *Journal of Personality and Social Psychology,* 1967, *5,* 202-210.

Sherif, M. Superordinate goals in the reduction of intergroup tensions. *American Journal of Sociology,* 1958, *53,* 349-356.

Sherman, A. *Behavior modification: Theory and practice.* Belmont, Calif.: Wadsworth Publishing Company, 1973.

Shumsky, A. *In search of teaching style.* New York: Appleton-Century-Crofts, 1968.

Sigel, I., and Coop, R. Cognitive style and classroom practice. In R.H. Coop and K. White (Eds.), *Psychological concepts in the classroom.* New York: Harper and Row, 1974.

Silberman, C. *Crisis in the classroom.* New York: Random House, 1970.

Simon, S., Howe, L., and Kirschenbaum, H. *Values clarification.* New York: Hart, 1972.

Simpson, B. *Becoming aware of values.* San Diego, Calif.: Pennant Press, 1973.

Simpson, R. Parental influence, anticipatory socialization, and social mobility. *American Sociological Review,* 1962, *27,* 517-522.

Sloane, H., Buckholdt, D., Jenson, W., and Crandall, J. *Structured teaching: A design for classroom management and instruction.* Champaign, Ill.: Research Press, 1979.

Sloggett, B. Use of group activities and team rewards to increase classroom productivity. *Teaching Exceptional Children,* 1971, *3,* 54-66.

Smith, I. *Spatial ability.* San Diego: Knapp, 1964.

Spaulding, R. Achievement, creativity, and self-concept correlates of teacher-pupil transactions in elementary schools. Urbana, Ill.: University of Illinois, Cooperative Research Project No. 1352, 1963.

Sperry, L. (Ed.). *Learning performance and individual differences.* Glenview, Ill.: Scott, Foresman, 1972.

Stallings, J. How instructional processes relate to child outcomes in a national study of follow-through. *Journal of Teacher Education,* 1976, *37,* 43-47.

Stallings, J., and Kaskowitz, D. *Follow-through classroom observation evaluation.* Menlo Park, California: Stanford Research Institute, 1974.

Stanford, G., and Stanford, B. *Learning discussion skills through games.* New York: Citation Press, 1969.

Stanwyck, D., and Felker, D. Self-concept and anxiety in middle elementary school children: A developmental survey. Paper presented at American Educational Research Association Convention, Chicago, 1974.

Stevens, D. Reading difficulty and classroom acceptance. *Reading Teacher,* 1971, *25,* 52-55.

Stinchcombe, A. *Rebellion in a high school.* Chicago: Quadrangle Books, 1964.

Stoffer, D. Investigation of positive behavioral changes as a function of genuineness, non-possessive warmth and empathic understanding. *Journal of Educational Research,* 1970, *63,* 225-228.

Sulzbacher, S., and Houser, J. A tactic to eliminate disruptive behaviors in a classroom: Group contingent consequences. *American Journal of Mental Deficiency,* 1968, *73,* 88-90.

Swift, M., and Spivack, G. *Alternative teaching strategies: Helping behaviorally troubled children achieve.* Champaign, Ill.: Research Press, 1975.

Tagiuri, R., Bruner, J., and Blake, R. On the relation between feelings and perception of feelings among members of small groups. In E. Maccoby, T. Newcomb, and E. Hartley (Eds.), *Readings in School Psychology.* New York: Holt, Rinehart and Winston, 1958.

Tanner, L. *Classroom discipline for effective teaching and learning.* New York: Holt, Rinehart and Winston, 1978.

Thomas, D., Becker, W., and Armstrong, M. Production and elimination of disruptive classroom behavior by systematically varying teacher's behavior. *Journal of Applied Behavior Analysis,* 1968, *1,* 35-45.

Tjosvold, D. Alternative organizations for schools and classrooms. In D. Bartel and L. Saxe (Eds.), *Social psychology of education: Research and theory.* New York: Hemisphere Press, 1977.

Tjosvold, D., and Santamaria, P. The effects of cooperation and teacher support on student attitudes toward classroom decision-making. Paper presented at American Educational Research Convention, New York, 1977.

Torgerson, E. What teenagers watch and why. *TV Guide,* April 23-29, 1977, 4-7.

Torrance, E. Explorations in creative thinking. *Education,* 1960, *81,* 216-220.

Travers, R. *Essentials of learning* (2nd ed.). New York: Macmillan, 1967.

Truax, C., and Carkhuff, R. *Toward effective counseling and psychotherapy: Training and practice.* Chicago: Aldine, 1967.

Truax, C., and Tatum, C. An extension from the effective psychotherapeutic model to constructive personality change in pre-school children. *Childhood Education,* 1966, *42,* 456-462.

Tuckman, B. Developmental sequence in small groups. *Psychological Bulletin,* 1965, *63,* 384-489.

Usher, R., and Hanke, J. The "third force" in psychology and college teacher effectiveness research at the University of Northern Colorado. *Colorado Journal of Educational Research,* 1971, *10,* 3-10.

Walberg, H., and Anderson, G. The achievement-creativity dimension and classroom climate. *Journal of Creative Behavior,* 1968, *2,* 281-292.

Walker, H. *The acting-out child: Coping with classroom disruption.* Boston: Allyn and Bacon, 1979.

Walker, H., and Buckley, N. *Token reinforcement techniques: Classroom applications for the hard-to-teach child.* Eugene, Oregon: E-P Press, Inc., 1974.

SUGGESTED READINGS

Walker, H., and Buckley, N. Teacher attention to appropriate and inappropriate classroom behavior: An individual case study. *Focus on Exceptional Children,* 1973, *5,* 5-11.

Walker, H., Hops, H., and Fiegenbaum, E. Deviant classroom behavior as a function of combination of social and token reinforcment and cost contingency. *Behavior Therapy,* 1976, *7,* 76-88.

Walker, H., Hops, H., Greenwood, C., Todd, N., and Garrett, B. The comparative effects of teacher praise, token reinforcement, and response cost in reducing negative peer interactions, CORBEH Report #25. Eugene, OR.: Center at Oregon for Research in the Behavioral Education of the Handicapped, University of Oregon; 1977.

Walker, H., Street, A., Garret, B., and Crossen, J. Experiments with response cost in playground and classroom settings. CORBEH Report No. 35. Eugene, Oregon: Center at Oregon for Research in the Behavioral Education of the Handicapped, University of Oregon, 1977.

Walters, R., Parke, R., and Cane, V. Timing of punishment and the observation of consequences to others as detriments of response inhibitions. *Journal of Experimental Child Psychology,* 1965, *2,* 10-30.

Ward, B., and Tikunoff, W. The effective teacher education program: Application of selected research results and methodology to teaching. *Journal of Teacher Education,* 1976, *27,* 58-53.

Warren, R., Deffenbacher, J., and Brading, P. Rational-emotive therapy and the reduction of test anxiety in elementary school students. *Rational Living,* 1976, (Fall), *11,* 26-29.

Watt, N. Longitudinal changes in the social behavior of children hospitalized for schizophrenia as adults. *Journal of Nervous and Mental Diseases,* 1972, *155,* 42-54.

Watt, N., Stolorowrd-Lubensky, A., and McClelland, D. Social adjustment and behavior of children hospitalized for schizophrenia as adults. *American Journal of Orthopsychiatry,* 1970, *40,* 637-657.

Weil, G., and Goldfried, M. Treatment of insomnia in an eleven-year-old child through self-relaxation. *Behavior Therapy,* 1973, *4,* 282-294.

Wheeler, R., and Ryan, F. Effects of cooperative and competitive classroom environments on the attitudes and achievement of elementary school students engaged in social studies inquiry activities. *Journal of Educational Psychology,* 1973, *65,* 402-407.

White, B., and Held, R. Plasticity of sensorimotor development in the human infant. In B. Staub and J. Hellmuth (Eds.), *Exceptional Infant, Vol. I.* Seattle: Special Child Publications, 1967, 425-442.

White, M. Natural rates of teacher approval and disapproval in the classroom. *Journal of Applied Behavior Analysis,* 1975, *8,* 367-372.

White, R. Motivation reconsidered: The concept of competence. *Psychological Review,* 1959, *66,* 297-333.

Williams, R., and Cole, S. Self-concept and adjustment. *Personnel and Guidance Journal,* 1968, *46,* 478-481.

Willis, B. The influence of teacher expectation on teachers' classroom interaction with selected children. *Dissertation Abstracts,* 1970, *30,* 5072-A.

Wilson, A. Residential segregation of social classes and aspirations of high school boys. *American Sociological Review,* 1959, *14,* 836-845.

Witkin, H., and Moore, C. Cognitive style and the teaching-learning process. Paper presented at the annual meeting of the American Educational Research Association, Chicago, April, 1974.

Wylie, R. *The self-concept.* Lincoln, University of Nebraska Press, 1961.

Wlodkowski, R. *Motivation and teaching: A practical guide.* Washington, D.C.: National Education Association, 1978.

Wolfgang, C., and Glickman, C. *Solving discipline problems: Strategies for classroom teachers.* Boston: Allyn and Bacon, 1980.

Yamamoto, K., Thomas, E., and Karnes, E. School related attitudes in middle-school age students. *American Educational Research Journal,* 1969, *6,* 191-206.

Yando, R., and Kagan, J. The effect of teacher tempo on the child. *Child Developement,* 1968, *39,* 27-34.

Nationwide teacher opinion poll. Washington, D.C.: National Education Assocation, 1979.

United States Department of Health, Education and Welfare, Public Health Service. Behavior patterns of children in school. Vital Health Statistics (J. Roberts and J. Baird, Jr.), 1972.